# Learning Culture through Reciting and Singing Classic Poems

# 吟唱古诗学文化

〔澳〕周晓康　编著
〔澳〕周晓康　T. Gourdon　译

By Dr. Xiaokang Zhou
Translated by Dr. Xiaokang Zhou & T. Gourdon

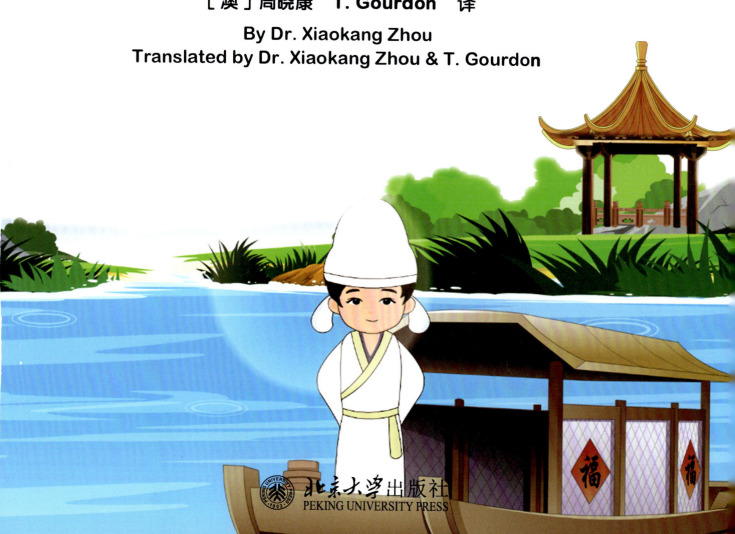

北京大学出版社
PEKING UNIVERSITY PRESS

图书在版编目(CIP)数据

吟唱古诗学文化：汉英对照 /（澳）周晓康编著. —北京：北京大学出版社，2020.7
ISBN 978-7-301-31118-9

Ⅰ.①吟… Ⅱ.①周… Ⅲ.①汉语–对外汉语教学–教材 Ⅳ.①H195.4

中国版本图书馆CIP数据核字（2020）第006093号

| | |
|---|---|
| 书　　　名 | 吟唱古诗学文化（汉英对照）<br>YINCHANG GUSHI XUE WENHUA (HAN-YING DUIZHAO) |
| 著作责任者 | ［澳］周晓康　编著 |
| 作　　　曲 | ［澳］周晓康 |
| 英文翻译 | ［澳］周晓康　T. Gourdon |
| 责任编辑 | 孙艳玲　任　蕾 |
| 标准书号 | ISBN 978-7-301-31118-9 |
| 出版发行 | 北京大学出版社 |
| 地　　　址 | 北京市海淀区成府路205号　100871 |
| 网　　　址 | http://www.pup.cn　新浪微博：@北京大学出版社 |
| 电子信箱 | zpup@pup.cn |
| 电　　　话 | 邮购部 010-62752015　发行部 010-62750672　编辑部 010-62753374 |
| 印刷者 | 北京宏伟双华印刷有限公司 |
| 经销者 | 新华书店<br>889毫米×1194毫米　16开　7印张　160千字<br>2020年7月第1版　2020年7月第1次印刷 |
| 定　　　价 | 98.00元（含动画、微课） |

未经许可，不得以任何方式复制或抄袭本书之部分或全部内容。
**版权所有，侵权必究**
举报电话：010-62752024　电子信箱：fd@pup.pku.edu.cn
图书如有印装质量问题，请与出版部联系，电话：010-62756370

# 序

晓康博士于1987至1989年期间曾在北京大学英语系攻读语言学方向的博士生课程，1998年在澳大利亚墨尔本大学获得语言学博士学位。2000年至今在墨尔本半岛文法学校从事汉语教学。晓康博士在澳大利亚的汉语教学中最突出的成就是编写了350余首语言教学歌谣，其中有不少已由北京大学出版社出版，如《晓康歌谣学汉语》《晓康歌谣学文化》《晓康歌谣趣味故事》等。

我本人有幸为她2012年出版的《丁丁迪米历险记》写过序。如今，晓康博士的新著《吟唱古诗学文化》又将出版。我注意到，两书相隔虽不久，国内外情况发生较多变化，确有不少新的感受，现与晓康和读者分享。

首先，当我为《丁丁迪米历险记》作序时，让我眼前一亮的是这是一本为中国学生写的课外读物，让中国学生熟悉澳大利亚的文化背景，使学生能了解英语国家中主流文化的一个重要侧面。现在却是另一种想法涌上心头，那就是我们不仅要让中国经济走出去，也要让中国文化走出去、让中国语言走出去。应该说，晓康博士的努力符合这个大方向。她用心编写了一本既提供诗歌中汉字的汉语拼音，也提供每个汉字的英文意义，最后提供全诗译文的教材，让学习者领悟和品味全诗的深层意义，从而了解中国文化。当然，编者也提供了如何进行教学的建议。我还想指出的是，这本教材不完全是针对国外学生的，它对国内学生也具有教学意义和文化价值。试想，如果中国学者和读者不掌握英文，又如何向国外朋友介绍中国文化，特别是古诗之美呢？

其次，这本教材反映了国内外教学思想的最新发展。我曾参加教育部有关《全日制义务教育英语课程标准》的编制和审订工作，但我的了解仅局限于对义务教育阶段的学生，应当引导学生在课堂上"听说唱游做"，等等。如今，晓康博士编的这本教材在教学理念上让我提高了一个台阶，那就是这本教材体现的当今时兴的多模态教育思想以及21世纪刚开展的

"微课"教学理念。两者充分体现于晓康博士在教材特色中所说的"在传统语言教材的基础上,借助音乐和动漫,将其发展成为融合型教材。诗歌配有动画和网络微课,包括中文朗诵、中文演唱和英文朗诵三个部分"。国人对多模态教育一般了解较多,对微课的概念比较生疏,因为它是最近十年才在国内迅速发展起来的教学模式。教育部在《教育信息化十年发展规划(2011—2020年)》中,提到要探索微课在课堂教与学创新应用中的有效模式和方法,挖掘和推广各地区的典型案例和先进经验,促进优质教育资源共建共享。晓康博士在教材特色中提到她是如何实践的,如"微课程……包括诗人及诗歌背景知识简介,生词、诗句的读音和语言点讲解,老师领读、学生跟读,老师领唱、学生跟唱,师生齐诵,师生齐唱,学生独诵,学生独唱,学生朗诵英文翻译,播放动画等十几个环节",这些都表明本教材的时代性、先进性,也表明晓康博士勇于探索和创新的精神。

最后,我们对这本教材的功能和价值的评价,不能仅限于把它看作是一本供海内外中小学学生使用的语言教材。从晓康博士的编写目标和过程,不难看出,她提供的既是精确押韵的英文翻译,也是朗朗上口的配乐吟唱。因此,本教材更可供中国高校英语专业和翻译专业学生、翻译老师、社会上的翻译工作者,以至翻译理论研究者阅读参考。

总的来说,晓康博士编著的《吟唱古诗学文化》是一本将中华优秀文化与先进教学理念结合,供海内外学习者使用的理想教材。

胡壮麟
北京大学外国语学院
2018年7月12日

# Foreword

Dr. Xiaokang Zhou studied the Ph. D. program in Linguistics in the Department of English of Peking (Beijing) University during 1987—1989, and was awarded the Doctoral degree in Linguistics in the University of Melbourne, Australia in 1998. She has been teaching Chinese in the Peninsula Grammar School since 2000. In her teaching of the Chinese language in Australia, Dr. Xiaokang Zhou's most outstanding achievements were her writing of more than 350 educational rhymes, many of which have been included in her books published by Peking University Press, such as *Dr. Zhou's Rhymes for Learning Chinese*, *Dr. Zhou's Rhymes for Learning Culture*, and *Dr. Zhou's Rhymes Fun Stories*, and etc..

I was fortunate enough to write the Foreword for her book *Adventures of Dingding and Damien* published in 2012. Now Dr. Xiaokang's new book *Learning Culture through Reciting and Singing Classic Poems* is to be published soon again. I noticed that it's not long time between the publication of these two books. During this period of time there have been quite a lot of changes in China, giving me many new ideas and thoughts which I would like to share with Xiaokang and her readers hereby.

First of all, when I wrote my Foreword for *Adventures of Dingding and Damien*, what attracted my eyes was that it was an after-school reader suitable for Chinese students to get to know Australia's background and to understand an important part of the main-stream culture of English-speaking countries. Now another idea came to my mind, that is, we should not only let the Chinese economy go out to the world, but also let the Chinese culture and language go out to the world. It is right to say that Dr. Xiaokang's effort is in line with this big picture—she thoughtfully edited these well-known classic Chinese poems and provided not only the Chinese *pinyin* (pronunciation-spelling) for each word/

character in the classic poems, but also provided the meaning of each word/character in English, and then provided the English translation of each poem for learners to understand and explore the deep meaning underneath, therefore to fully understand the Chinese culture. Of course, the author has also provided advice as to how to teach these poems. What I also want to point out is this book is not just for foreign students overseas, it is more relevant and meaningful to students in China, in learning these poems, together with the cultural value presented. Imagine, if Chinese scholars and readers do not have a good grasp of English, how can they introduce the Chinese culture to foreign friends, particularly the beauty of classic Chinese poems?

Secondly, this textbook with its flash videos and online micro-lessons shows the latest developments in the teaching pedagogy both at home and abroad. I was once involved in the editing and examining *the Standards of English Course in the Full-time Compulsory Education*, yet I only knew that for students in the compulsory education, they should be instructed to practise "listening, speaking, singing, playing and doing" in class, and so on. But now, this textbook together with its teaching resources led me to another level upward with regard to the new concepts of teaching, that is, this textbook represents the current model of Multimodal Education, as well as the use of micro-lesson that has just come into being in the 21$^{st}$ century. They are fully reflected in what Dr. Xiaokang wrote about the features of this textbook: "In addition to the traditional textbook, it is a kind of integrated textbook with the help of music and cartoon presentation. Some poems form a lesson which is composed of an online lecture and a flash cartoon video including a speaking and singing version in Chinese and a speaking version in English."

In China, people know more about the Multimodal Education, but less about the micro-lecture, because the latter has only developed rapidly in China over the past 10 years. In *the 10-Year Development Plan of Digital Education (2011—2020)*, the Ministry of Education urges us to explore effective models and methods of using micro-lesson in the classroom teaching and innovative application, discover and promote typical cases and advanced experiences in various areas, to facilitate creating and sharing excellent quality educational resources. Dr. Xiaokang outlined her practice in the features of this textbook: "Each poem has over 10 short steps: a brief introduction about the poet and relevant historical and natural background, followed by the explanation of the new words and expressions/sentences, their pronunciation and grammatical points, reading and singing by the teacher and student, separately and together, and watching the flash video." These show the updated trend of the times and advanced qualities of this textbook together with its supporting resources, and also demonstrate Dr. Xiaokang's inquisitive and innovative courage and spirit.

Finally, when evaluating the functions and value of this textbook, we should not limit it to that of a language textbook for primary and middle/high school students only. From her editing purpose and production progress of this textbook, we can see clearly that Dr. Xiaokang Zhou has provided not only musical chanting of the poems, but also accurate and rhythmical English translation, and therefore this textbook can be used by university teachers and students majoring in English and Translation, professional translators and researchers in translation theories in China, as a reference book.

All in all, *Learning Culture through Reciting and Singing Classic Poems* produced by Dr. Xiaokang Zhou is an ideal textbook for learners both in China and overseas, with its strong combination of the wonderfully rich Chinese culture and advanced and novel teaching methodology.

Zhuanglin Hu<br>
School of Foreign languages, Peking University<br>
12/7/2018<br>
Translated by Xiaokang Zhou

# 自 序

2018至2019年有几个数字意义非凡，令人思绪万千。

可以说，2018年是我人生中迄今为止最值得纪念的一年。1977年中国恢复高考，77、78级于1978年考入大学，我是其中一员，至此40周年；1987年我被北京大学录取，攻读西方语言学博士学位，至此31周年；1997年我完成墨尔本大学语言学博士论文，1998年获得墨尔本大学博士学位，至此20周年；2008年我在澳大利亚的海外汉语教学中开发的汉语歌谣教材《晓康歌谣学汉语》正式出版，至此10周年。2019年同样值得纪念，这一年是我在澳大利亚移民定居30周年，也是我在墨尔本半岛文法学校任教20周年。多么有意义的几个数字！"十年磨一剑"，一路走来，从国内到国外，从理论到实践，见证了我在求知、科研、教学途中的每一个脚步，每一份收获。如今，北京大学出版社即将出版的这本《吟唱古诗学文化》，又是一份对汉语言文学及中华文化教学的创新，其中也饱含着海外汉语教师对传播中华文化的满腔热情与勤奋努力，以及学生们学有所获的喜悦与欣慰。

在此，我要衷心地感谢本套教材制作团队每个成员的辛勤付出和大家的精诚合作：

微课主讲：周晓康（中英文），徐林、李林蓓（中文）

作　　曲：周晓康

音乐合成：深圳索亚文化传播有限公司

中文演唱：黄薇薇、黄美婷、杨晓玲、方雄、范文芳、周晓康

中文朗诵：魏青、徐林、范文芳、周晓康

学生演唱、朗诵：Arden Baker, Oliver Woodman, James Woodland, Jaye Marchiandi, James Logan, Holly Gray, Samantha Robison

英文翻译：周晓康、Tim Gourdon

英文朗诵：Sue, Robert Savige, Robin Du-Gourdon, Teisha King, Monique Fagioli, 周晓康

动画/微课制作：深圳帧格文化传播有限公司

出品人：周晓康

  同时，我也要衷心感谢我的北大导师胡壮麟教授亲自为本书作序，并对教材给予了高度的评价。最后，我还要向这些年里所有支持我、帮助我的同行们、朋友们、家长们、学生们致以最诚挚的谢意！感恩一路有你们的陪伴和鼓励！

  我衷心期待本教材及其微课课程能给广大读者带来学习古诗和中华文化全新的体验和乐趣，让我们在汲取古人的智慧与才华中尽情享受，即兴吟诵那超凡脱俗、清新隽永的优美诗句、千古绝唱。

周晓康

于墨尔本

2019年12月31日

# The Author's Foreword

2018—2019 presents several significant numbers that bring up overwhelmingly emotional reminiscence of my life's journey, and now looking forward I see more exciting time ahead.

It can be said that 2018 was the most rememberable year in my life. With the re-establishment of the university entry examination system in China in 1977, students of Classes 1977 and 1978 who passed the examinations were enrolled in various universities in 1978—I was one of them—it was the 40th Anniversary. In 1987 I was accepted by Peking University to study Western Linguistics with a Ph. D. degree—it was the 31st Anniversary. I completed my Ph. D. thesis in Linguistics at the University of Melbourne, Australia in 1997 and was granted the Doctor of Philosophy degree in Linguistics of Melbourne University in 1998—it was the 20th Anniversary. In 2008 my Chinese rhyme textbooks (*Dr. Zhou's Rhymes for Learning Chinese*) that I wrote and developed while teaching Chinese to non-native speakers in Australia were published, hence the 10th Anniversary separately. 2019 is also memorable, which is the 30th Anniversary of my immigration to and settlement in Australia. And also it is the 20th Anniversary of my teaching at Peninsula Grammar in Melbourne. What significant numbers they are! As a well-known Chinese idiom says "Grinding a sword for 10 years", these figures witnessed every step I took and every harvest I achieved on my journey from China to Australia, from theoretical studies to professional practice, from rhymes and songs to music composition in learning, researching, teaching and career pursuing, academic and educational. Now, this textbook *Learning Culture through Reciting and Singing Classic Chinese Poems* to be published by Peking University Press very soon, is another innovation to the teaching of Chinese language and culture. It sees the great enthusiasm and hard work of the Chinese teachers in our Chinese classes overseas to promote our Chinese language and culture, as well as the happiness and pleasure of the students derived from its excellent learning outcomes.

I would like to hereby express my heart-felt gratitude to every member of our great team for their extraordinary hard work and sincere co-operation:

**Chief Lecturer**: Xiaokang Zhou (English-Chinese)
Lin Xu (Chinese), Linbei Li (Chinese)

**Composer**: Xiaokang Zhou

**Music Maker**: Shenzhen Suoya Culture Promotion Co. Ltd.

**Chinese Singing**: Weiwei Huang, Meiting Huang, Xiaoling Yang, Xiong Fang, Wenfang Fan, Xiaokang Zhou

**Chinese Reciting**: Qing Wei, Lin Xu, Wenfang Fan, Xiaokang Zhou

**Student Singing and Reciting**: Arden Baker, Oliver Woodman, James Woodland, Jaye Marchiandi, James Logan, Holly Gray, Samantha Robison

**English Translation**: Xiaokang Zhou, Tim Gourdon

**English Reciting**: Sue, Robert Savige, Robin Du-Gourdon, Teisha King, Monique Fagioli, Xiaokang Zhou

**Flash Video and Micro-lesson Maker**: Shenzhen Zhenge Culture Promotion Co. Ltd.

**Producer**: Xiaokang Zhou

At the same time, I would also like to thank Professor Hu Zhuanglin, my Peking University Ph. D. study supervisor for writing the Foreword to this book and for his kind words and positive comments on its main features. Last but not the least, I would like to extend my sincere gratitude to all my colleagues, friends, students and their parents who have supported and helped me continuously over these years. Thank you very much for your company and encouragement all the way through!

I hope from the bottom of my heart that this set of textbook and its related micro-lessons will bring to the readers a brand new and exciting experience together with the pleasure of learning the classic Chinese poems and culture. Let's enjoy reciting and singing these superbly beautiful, profoundly simple and ever-lasting unique poems while absorbing the wisdom and talent of the ancient Chinese poets.

Xiaokang Zhou<br/>Melbourne<br/>31/12/2019

# 前　言

　　本教材源于作者多年来在海外汉语教学一线从事语言和文化教学的探索和实践。全书收入中国古典诗歌（唐、宋、清）33首，由作者周晓康博士谱曲，并与《丁丁迪米历险记》的合著者Tim Gourdon先生一起翻译成英文版。该教材可在中小学汉语课堂中用作学习中华文化的辅助教学，还可为中国诗歌朗诵比赛提供诗歌教学并作为比赛内容。

**教材特色**

　　在传统语言教材的基础上，借助音乐和动漫，将其发展成为融合型教材。诗歌配有动画和网络微课，包括中文朗诵、中文演唱和英文朗诵三个部分。微课程有助于老师教学和学生自学，其中包括诗人及诗歌背景知识简介，生词、诗句的读音和语言点讲解，老师领读、学生跟读，老师领唱、学生跟唱，师生齐诵，师生齐唱，学生独诵，学生独唱，学生朗诵英文翻译，播放动画等十几个环节。全课采用汉英对照形式讲授，图文并茂，通过朗诵、演唱、视频等全方位的学习途径和体验，增加学生的学习兴趣和学习热情，扩大学生的知识面和词汇量，提升学生的语言文化修养和综合运用能力。

　　教材另一特色在于其英文翻译，理解到位，用词精确，合辙押韵，朗朗上口，每一首古诗都是一首地道的英文诗歌，堪称中西合璧，从而给英语作为第二语言的学习者带来地道的英文和愉悦的学习体验。

**适用对象**

　　1. 中国的中小学生和国际学校学生，既学古诗，又学英语；

　　2. 海外中文作为第二语言的学生（从小学生到中学生、大学生，从初学者到中、高级水平学生），学习中国古典诗歌的语言和文学要素；

　　3. 国内外中小学和大学对外汉语教师，既可以提高自己对古诗的理解和修养，尤其是用英语讲解每首诗歌的内容和形式，又可以直接拿来教学，吸引学生的注意力，提高学生的学习兴趣和热情；

4. 中国高校英语专业、翻译专业的学生和教师以及翻译工作者，用作翻译教程或范文，其亮点是经典的古诗加地道的古诗英文翻译。

**选材说明**

教材所选古代诗歌，大多和海外汉语教学课程的话题相关，比如《吟雪》，以学习、复习学生所学的汉语数字和量词为主；《咏鹅》《绝句》可以结合课程中的动物和颜色这两个话题；《回乡偶书》《静夜思》《游子吟》《九月九日忆山东兄弟》等可以表达乡情、亲情等主题，与家庭、亲人等话题和词汇挂钩；《春晓》《草》《清明》《春夜喜雨》《悯农》《江雪》《枫桥夜泊》《长安秋望》《望月怀远》《咏柳》《梅花》《春望》《忆江南》等可以与气候、四季、节日、自然景物、风土人情等话题和词汇结合起来；《相思》《无题》《别董大》《送灵澈》《赠汪伦》《黄鹤楼送孟浩然之广陵》《海内存知己》等可结合爱情、友情等话题和相关的表达；《早发白帝城》《登鹳雀楼》《望庐山瀑布》《黄鹤楼》《登幽州台歌》《马诗》等可以与旅游、观光、历史等主题相关联。而大多数诗歌的意境、立意都有相同之处，可以用来激励学生了解中国传统文化和价值观，既长见识又励志。

考虑到学习者的汉语水平与课堂教学效果，部分篇幅长、难度大的诗歌我们节选一部分，如《春夜喜雨》；或对标题进行更改，如《赋得古原草送别》，节选后改为《草》。

**学习效果**

通常一节课的学习就能使学生学到二三十个生词和四五个句型，掌握这些词语和句子的发音、声调，并能吟唱全诗。与传统的语言教学相比，课文内容和学习效果更胜一筹，传统课堂每节课的教学质量与学习效果难以达到诗歌（歌谣）形式的教学所能达到的目标。并且，最重要的是学生在短短一节课里因其所学到的语言及文化知识而产生强烈的成就感远高于传统课堂教学。

# Preface

This book originates from the author's many years of teaching practices of the Chinese language and culture in the forefront of classroom education overseas. It collects 33 classic Chinese poems (from Tang, Song and Qing Dynasties), with music composed by the author (Dr. Xiaokang Zhou) and translated into English by the author and the co-author Tim Gourdon of *Adventures of Dingding and Damien*. This book can be used as a supplementary teaching material for non-native speakers to learn about the Chinese culture and to provide the poetry texts for the Chinese poetry recital competition.

**Features**

In addition to the traditional textbook, it is a kind of integrated textbook with the help of music and cartoon presentation. Some poems form a lesson which is composed of an online lecture and a flash cartoon video including a speaking and singing version in Chinese and a speaking version in English. The online micro-lesson course helps teachers to teach, and students to learn easily and at their own pace, each poem has over 10 short steps: a brief introduction about the poet and relevant historical and natural background, followed by the explanation of the new words and expressions/sentences, their pronunciation and grammatical points, reading and singing by the teacher and students, separately and together, and watching the flash video. The whole course is conducted in Chinese and English, with beautiful and vivid pictures, music, recitation, singing and video watching, which provides a new and happy learning experience for the audience, draws their attention and increases their interests and enthusiasm in learning. It also broadens their knowledge and enlarges their vocabulary, consolidating their

understanding of the language and culture/literature and improving their over-all linguistic ability and communication skills.

Another important feature of this book is its English translation of each poem, with accurate understanding and interpretation, precise and sophisticated use of the vocabulary and rhythmical technique. Learners may experience a feeling of pleasure when reciting these poems. The translation of each poem has been adapted to English in poetical form, quite naturally and well matched between the Oriental and Western cultures. It can also give students in China and the non-native speakers of English overseas an authentic, classic, easy and pleasant experience and a sense of achievement in learning English.

**Suitable Readers**

1. Young children and middle school and international school students in China to learn not only the classic Chinese poems but also English;

2. Chinese as a second language students overseas (from primary schools, middle/high schools to universities, from beginners to intermediate and advanced levels) to learn the classic Chinese poems and the embedded linguistic and cultural elements;

3. Primary, middle/high school and university Chinese teachers, both in China or overseas, not only to improve their understanding and appreciation of the classic Chinese poems, especially to analyze and explain the content of the poems in English, but also to use these resources in their own teaching to keep their students interested and engaged with enthusiasm;

4. University students and teachers majoring in English and Translation and others specialised in Translation, who can use this book as their textbook or translation model work, as these are the authentic classic poems including a truly adaptable translation.

**About the Selection of the Poems**

The classic Chinese poems selected in this book are closely related to the themes and topics of our classroom teaching of the Chinese language and

culture course, including the vocabulary and grammar. For example, *An Ode to Snowflakes*, can help students to learn and revise the numbers and measure words that they have learned; *An Ode to the Goose*, and *A Four-line Poem* can be combined with the topics of animals and colours in the course content; *Return to Hometown, Quiet Night Thoughts, A Travelling Son's Chant* and *Remembering Shandong Brothers on 9$^{th}$ of 9$^{th}$* show the feelings about one's hometown and relatives and can be used in teaching the topics and vocabulary about family and relatives; *Spring Dawn, Prairie Grass, Qingming Festival, Spring Night Happy Rain, Saluting the Farmer, Snow on the River, Maple Bridge Night Mooring, Autumn View in Chang'an, Moonlight Thoughts, An Ode to the Willow, Plum Blossoms, Spring Watch* and *Recalling River South* can be used to teach the topics and vocabulary about weather, seasons, festivals, natural landscape and scenery, customs and human emotions; *Thinking of Each Other, Untitled, Farewell to Dong Da, On Parting with Lingche, To Wang Lun, A Farewell at Yellow Crane Pagoda* and *Bosom Friends across the Seas* fit very well with the topics and relevant expressions about love and friendship; *Early Morning Leaving White King City, Climbing the Stork Pagoda, Watching the Waterfall on Mount Lu, Yellow Crane Pagoda, Climbing Youzhou Pagoda* and *An Ode to the Horse* are relevant to the topics of tourism, sightseeing and history. Most of these poems have similar morals and artistic aspirations that can inspire students to explore and understand the tradition of the Chinese culture and value system, broadening their vision and lifting their spirits.

Considering the Chinese level of learners and the effect of teaching, we select part of the poem as a lesson, such as *Spring Night Happy Rain*, or change the title, such as *Prairie Grass*.

**The Learning Effect and Outcome**

It takes only one lesson for students to learn 20-30 new words and 4-5 grammatical structures and their pronunciation and tones, and to read and sing the whole poem, most of the time, with short 4-line poems. This is very different from the traditional teaching methodology in terms of the content and learning outcomes. It is obviously more effective and productive, while the latter is usually limited in its teaching content and learning outcome, and it is difficult to achieve what has been achieved through the use of poems and rhymes. More importantly, the sense of achievement derived and shown by students from learning so much and gaining so much insight into the language and culture in a short lesson is truly remarkable and beyond comparison.

# C 目录 ontent

1. 吟雪　An Ode to Snowflakes ／ 1
2. 咏鹅　An Ode to the Goose ／ 3
3. 回乡偶书　Return to Hometown ／ 5
4. 静夜思　Quiet Night Thoughts ／ 7
5. 春晓　Spring Dawn ／ 9

6. 游子吟　A Travelling Son's Chant ／ 11
7. 早发白帝城　Early Morning Leaving White King City ／ 13

8. 草　Prairie Grass ／ 15
9. 登鹳雀楼　Climbing the Stork Pagoda ／ 17

10. 绝句　A Four-line Poem ／ 19
11. 相思　Thinking of Each Other ／ 21
12. 无题　Untitled ／ 23

13. 清明　Qingming Festival ／ 25
14. 春夜喜雨　Spring Night Happy Rain ／ 27
15. 悯农　Saluting the Farmer ／ 29

16. 望庐山瀑布　Watching the Waterfall on Mount Lu ／ 31

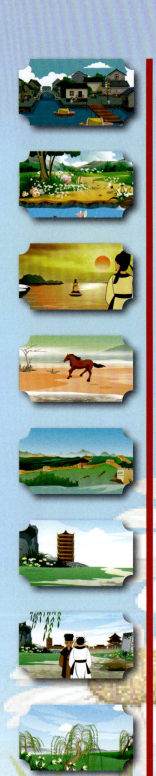

17. 江雪　Snow on the River ／ 33

18. 枫桥夜泊　Maple Bridge Night Mooring ／ 35

19. 长安秋望　Autumn View in Chang'an ／ 37

20. 九月九日忆山东兄弟　Remembering Shandong Brothers on 9th of 9th ／ 39

21. 望月怀远　Moonlight Thoughts ／ 41

22. 别董大　Farewell to Dong Da ／ 43

23. 送灵澈　On Parting with Lingche ／ 45

24. 赠汪伦　To Wang Lun ／ 47

25. 咏柳　An Ode to the Willow ／ 49

26. 梅花　Plum Blossoms ／ 51

27. 春望　Spring Watch ／ 53

28. 黄鹤楼送孟浩然之广陵　A Farewell at Yellow Crane Pagoda ／ 55

29. 黄鹤楼　Yellow Crane Pagoda ／ 57

30. 登幽州台歌　Climbing Youzhou Pagoda ／ 59

31. 马诗　An Ode to the Horse ／ 61

32. 忆江南　Recalling River South ／ 63

33. 海内存知己　Bosom Friends across the Seas ／ 65

词语表 ／ 67

Vocabulary ／ 67

作者简介 ／ 86

About the Author ／ 88

## 吟 雪
### An Ode to Snowflakes

纪 昀 （1724—1805）

一片两片三四片，
one | piece | two | piece | three | four | piece

五片六片七八片，
five | piece | six | piece | seven | eight | piece

九片十片千万片，
nine | piece | ten | piece | thousand | ten thousand | piece

飞入芦花皆不见。
fly | into | reed | flower | all | not | see

### An Ode to Snowflakes

*Ji Yun*

One snowflake two snowflakes three snowflakes four,
five snowflakes six snowflakes seven eight and more,
nine snowflakes ten snowflakes thousands, more and more;
Drifting down onto the reed flowers by the score,
never to be seen again as on the earth they thaw.

(*Translated by Dr. X. Zhou & T. Gourdon*)

In this poem, the poet depicts a calm and pure world of snow falling from the sky and floating into the water mixing with the reed flowers. He enjoyed watching the snowflakes falling around him and started counting them one by one like a child cheerfully, as he was amazed by the power of nature as shown in the falling snowflakes melting into the water as they disappeared, and on the other hand the poet may have felt sorry for the fallen snowflakes, but he did not want to show this directly, instead he focused on the positive and good side of this natural phenomenon by lightly describing the scene of the snowflakes mingling with the reed flowers as if they were still alive and were visiting the reeds in their territory or taking another form of life now, on the ground, in the water rather than in the sky, or from the heaven.

Perhaps the poet sees the snowflakes as a cycle of life. The snowflakes began as water and after a brief existence above, floated down from the sky and became water again perhaps to return one day as a snowflake.

*By Dr. X. Zhou*

## yǒng é
# 咏鹅
### An Ode to the Goose

luò bīn wáng
骆宾王（约638—684）

é  é  é
**鹅 鹅 鹅，**
goose | goose | goose

qū xiàng xiàng tiān gē
**曲 项 向 天 歌。**
bending | neck | towards | sky | sing

bái máo fú lǜ shuǐ
**白 毛 浮 绿 水，**
white | feather | float | green | water

hóng zhǎng bō qīng bō
**红 掌 拨 清 波。**
red | palm | paddle | clear | wave

## An Ode to the Goose
*Luo Binwang*

Goose, goose, goose,
bending neck skyward to sing.
White feather drifting on green water,
red feet paddling over clear waves in spring.

(*Translated by Dr. X. Zhou & T. Gourdon*)

In this poem the poet is giving his first impression of a goose he saw in a pond. It was a very vivid description of the goose in terms of the colours and the clear water, as well as the happiness of the moment when the goose is singing his own song to the sky. What is special about this poem is that this was the first poem the poet wrote when he was only 7 years old. It showed his poetic genius.

*By Dr. X. Zhou*

## huí xiāng ǒu shū
# 回乡偶书
### Return to Hometown

hè zhī zhāng
贺知章（659—744）

shào xiǎo lí jiā lǎo dà huí
**少小离家老大回，**
young | little | leave | home | old | big | return

xiāng yīn wú gǎi bìn máo cuī
**乡音无改鬓毛衰。**
native | accent | not | change | temples | hair | turn grey

ér tóng xiāng jiàn bù xiāng shí
**儿童相见不相识，**
son | child | each other | meet | not | each other | know

xiào wèn kè cóng hé chù lái
**笑问客从何处来。**
smile | ask | guest | from | which | place | come

# Return to Hometown

*He Zhizhang*

Young boy left home,
and returned as adult fully grown,
accent unchanged, hair on temples grey.
Children don't know this person from far away,
smilingly they ask: where are you from?
We have not seen you before today.

*(Translated by Dr. X. Zhou & T. Gourdon)*

This poem illustrates the poet's deep feeling for his hometown and nostalgic mood on return. He uses very simple words and expressions to show the deep emotions of someone returning home after a long time away.

*By Dr. X. Zhou*

<sup>jìng yè sī</sup>
# 静夜思
## Quiet Night Thoughts

<sup>lǐ</sup> <sup>bái</sup>
李 白（701—762）

<sup>chuáng qián míng yuè guāng</sup>
**床 前 明 月 光，**
bed | front | bright | moon | light

<sup>yí shì dì shàng shuāng</sup>
**疑 是 地 上 霜。**
doubt | be | ground | on | frost

<sup>jǔ tóu wàng míng yuè</sup>
**举 头 望 明 月，**
raise | head | look at | bright | moon

<sup>dī tóu sī gù xiāng</sup>
**低 头 思 故 乡。**
lower | head | think | old | hometown

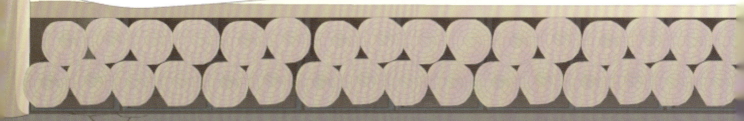

### Quiet Night Thoughts

*Li Bai*

Bright moon shining beside my bed,
I wonder if it is frost on the ground.
So raising my head,
I see the moon shining bright,
lowering my head, I think of my hometown out of sight.

(*Translated by Dr. X. Zhou & T. Gourdon*)

This poem expresses a deep feeling for one's family and hometown. The poet captures his thoughts in a moment of consciousness between sleep and dreams, seeing the bright moon light in front of his bed as a symbol of family reunification shared by all, and produces this short but very real to us all poem.

*By Dr. X. Zhou*

## chūn xiǎo
## 春 晓
**Spring Dawn**

mèng hào rán
孟 浩 然（689—740）

chūn mián bù jué xiǎo
**春 眠 不 觉 晓，**
spring | sleep | not | aware of | dawn

chù chù wén tí niǎo
**处 处 闻 啼 鸟。**
everywhere | hear | sing | bird

yè lái fēng yǔ shēng
**夜 来 风 雨 声，**
night | come | wind | rain | sound

huā luò zhī duō shǎo
**花 落 知 多 少？**
flower | fall | know | how many

### Spring Dawn
*Meng Haoran*

Spring sleep unaware of dawn,
birds singing everywhere as the day is reborn.
With the night came the sound of wind and rain,
how many flowers fell, will they bloom again?
(*Translated by Dr. X. Zhou & T. Gourdon*)

In this poem, the poet grasps a small but often missed part of a day while many of us sleep through the night and dawn, on awakening we may look outside to see what changes spring has brought. He also expresses his deep sympathy for the flowers falling in the rain, blown away by the wind.

*By Dr. X. Zhou*

## yóu zǐ yín
## 游子吟
**A Travelling Son's Chant**

mèng jiāo
孟 郊（751—814）

cí mǔ shǒu zhōng xiàn
**慈母手中线，**
kind | mother | hand | in | thread

yóu zǐ shēn shàng yī
**游子身上衣。**
travel | son | body | on | clothes

lín xíng mì mì féng
**临行密密缝，**
before | journey | tight | tight | knit

yì kǒng chí chí guī
**意恐迟迟归。**
mind | afraid | late | late | return

shuí yán cùn cǎo xīn
**谁言寸草心，**
who | say | inch | grass | heart

bào dé sān chūn huī
**报得三春晖。**
return | get | three | spring | sunshine

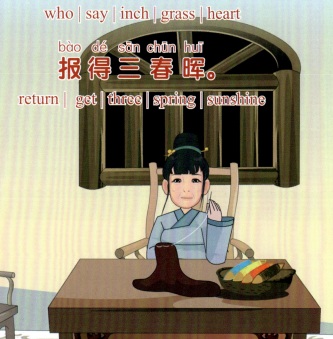

### A Travelling Son's Chant

*Meng Jiao*

Kind mother's hand sewing the threads,
for a travelling son's leaving that she dreads.
Before his journey she's casting tight knit threads,
afraid he will not return soon, her heart torn in shreds.
Who says a tiny heart of a baby's, light as a blade of grass, can repay
the spring sunshine as warm as his mother's love for him everyday.

(*Translated by Dr. X. Zhou & T. Gourdon*)

This poem expresses the greatest love in the world of a mother to her child. The poet really delves deeply into the emotions of a mother whose son she has long loved and cared for, leaves home for the first time. She ponders: Will I ever see him again? This thought is written between the lines. An extremely sensitive observation by the poet. The kindness of a mother is irreplaceable and unmeasurable.

*By Dr. X. Zhou*

## 早发白帝城
### Early Morning Leaving White King City

李 白 (701—762)

zhāo cí bái dì cǎi yún jiān
朝辞白帝彩云间，
morning | farewell | white | king | colourful | cloud | among

qiān lǐ jiāng líng yí rì huán
千里江陵一日还。
thousand | mile | river | hill | one | day | return

liǎng àn yuán shēng tí bú zhù
两岸猿声啼不住，
two | bank | ape | sound | cry | not | stop

qīng zhōu yǐ guò wàn chóng shān
轻舟已过万重山。
light | boat | already | pass | ten thousand | layer | mountain

## Early Morning Leaving White King City
*Li Bai*

Early morning farewell to White King City under colourful clouds,
a thousand miles to River Hill Town in one day.
Apes calling non-stop on the river banks along the way,
light boat already passed ten thousand mountains today.

(*Translated by Dr. X. Zhou & T. Gourdon*)

This poem expresses the feelings of someone leaving a place of tranquillity in the silence of dawn alone in a small boat with only the call of the apes on the river banks to keep him company. The poet thoroughly enjoys the serenity and tranquillity of nature.

*By Dr. X. Zhou*

## 草
### Prairie Grass

白居易 (772—846)

离离原上草,
clearly | prairie | on | grass

一岁一枯荣。
one | year | once | die | flourish

野火烧不尽,
wild | fire | burn | not | end

春风吹又生。
spring | wind | blow | again | grow

### Prairie Grass

*Bai Juyi*

Clear prairie abundant with grass,
one year die, next year flourish.
Wild fire burn, grass never perish,
spring wind blow, grass again grow.
(*Translated by Dr. X. Zhou & T. Gourdon*)

    This poem points out the cycle of life as reflected in the changing seasons in nature and the resilience of life on earth. Even wild fire cannot stop grasses from regenerating.

*By Dr. X. Zhou*

## 登鹳雀楼
### Climbing the Stork Pagoda

王之涣 (688—742)

bái rì yī shān jìn
**白日依山尽,**
white | sun | along | mountain | end

huáng hé rù hǎi liú
**黄 河 入 海 流。**
yellow | river | enter | sea | flow

yù qióng qiān lǐ mù
**欲 穷 千 里 目,**
want | see | thousand | mile | view

gèng shàng yì céng lóu
**更 上 一 层 楼。**
more | climb up | one | storey | building

### Climbing the Stork Pagoda
*Wang Zhihuan*

White sun at mountains' end,
follows the Yellow River's seaward trend.
To have a thousand miles view,
climb higher and think anew.

(*Translated by Dr. X. Zhou & T. Gourdon*)

This poem delivers a positive message about aiming high and pursuing your ambitions to the full. The poet describes the natural beauty of the scenery of the Yellow River and the mountains and then points out that the higher you climb up, the more you can see, which implies that you will get a better return for your efforts.

*By Dr. X. Zhou*

## 绝句 (jué jù)
### A Four-line Poem

杜甫（dù fǔ）(712—770)

liǎng gè huáng lí míng cuì liǔ
**两个黄鹂鸣翠柳，**
two | measure word | yellow | oriole | sing | green | willow

yì háng bái lù shàng qīng tiān
**一行白鹭上青天。**
one | line | white | egret | fly up | blue | sky

chuāng hán xī lǐng qiān qiū xuě
**窗含西岭千秋雪，**
window | embrace | west | hill | thousand | autumn | snow

mén bó dōng wú wàn lǐ chuán
**门泊东吴万里船。**
door | moor | east | Wu | ten thousand | mile | boat

# A Four-line Poem

*Du fu*

Two yellow orioles in green willows sing,
across the blue sky a line of white egrets soar on wing.
Window's view embraces west mountains thousand years snows,
river door to East wu Kingdom moor boats
from ten thousand miles away lights aglow.

(*Translated by Dr. X. Zhou and T. Gourdon*)

This poem captures a serenity of the countryside beside a river where there are green willows and beautiful birds, and the vivid blue sky with snow-capped mountains and boats moored on the water which were from the East Wu Kingdom. It shows the poet's appreciation of nature's beauty.

*By Dr. X. Zhou*

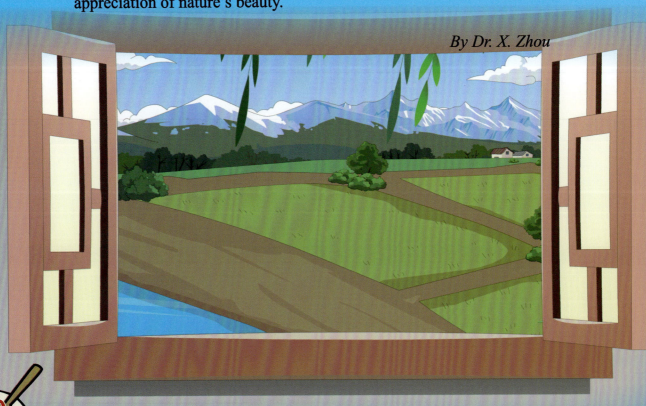

## 11. 相思 (xiāng sī)
### Thinking of Each Other

王维 (wáng wéi) (701—761)

红豆生南国，
hóng dòu shēng nán guó
red | bean | grow | south | country

春来发几枝。
chūn lái fā jǐ zhī
spring | come | shoot | a few | branch

愿君多采撷，
yuàn jūn duō cǎi xié
wish | you | more | pick up

此物最相思。
cǐ wù zuì xiāng sī
this | thing | most | each other | think

# Thinking of Each Other
*Wang Wei*

Red beans grow in the South,

spring shoots on branches reach out.

Please pick as many as you may,

they express my love for you in every way.

(*Translated by Dr. X. Zhou and T. Gourdon*)

This is a simple poem with deep meaning and profound love. The red beans represent one's feelings for the loved ones. The spring shows life and love in nature, the beauty of the world we live in, and hence, happiness.

*By Dr. X. Zhou*

# 12

## 无题
### Untitled

李商隐（约813—约858）

相见时难别亦难，
each other | meet | time | difficult | farewell | also | difficult

东风无力百花残。
east | wind | no | strength | hundred | flower | wither

春蚕到死丝方尽，
spring | silkworm | until | die | silk | just | end

蜡炬成灰泪始干。
wax | torch | become | ash | tears | begin | dry

# Untitled

*Li Shangyin*

Meet loved ones deep emotions quiver,
leave loved ones feelings again rise high.
East wind weakens and flowers wither,
spring silkworm spins until death comes hither,
wax candle burns to ash and tears dry.

(*Translated by Dr. X. Zhou and T. Gourdon*)

This poem points out the importance of relationships and the ever-lasting power of love, just like silkworms that never give up until they spin the last silk thread, and also candles that burn to ashes. The last two sentences of this poem have been quoted many times throughout the history to inspire people to become selfless and work hard for the country.

*By Dr. X. Zhou*

## 清 明
### Qingming Festival

杜 牧 (803—852)

**qīng míng shí jié yǔ fēn fēn**
清 明 时 节 雨 纷 纷，
clear | bright | time | season | rain | in succession

**lù shàng xíng rén yù duàn hún**
路 上 行 人 欲 断 魂。
road | on | walk | people | almost | lose | soul

**jiè wèn jiǔ jiā hé chù yǒu**
借 问 酒 家 何 处 有？
borrow | ask | wine | home | which | place | have

**mù tóng yáo zhǐ xìng huā cūn**
牧 童 遥 指 杏 花 村。
shepherd | child | far | point | apricot | blossom | village

## Qingming Festival

*Du Mu*

Qingming Festival under drizzling rain drops,
people on the road almost lose their spirit as soul flops.
Where is the nearest inn?
Shepherd boy points to Apricot Blossom Village within.

*(Translated by Dr. X. Zhou & T. Gourdon)*

This is a poem about the Qingming Festival which falls mostly on the 4th or 5th of April. On this day, people make a pilgrimage to their ancestors or loved ones in resting places. The poet lightens the mood by referring to an inn and a cheerful village named Apricot Blossom.

*By Dr. X. Zhou*

## 春夜喜雨
### Spring Night Happy Rain

杜 甫(dù fǔ)(712—770)

hǎo yǔ zhī shí jié
**好雨知时节,**
good | rain | know | time | season

dāng chūn nǎi fā shēng
**当春乃发生。**
when | spring | then | happen

suí fēng qián rù yè
**随风潜入夜,**
follow | wind | dive | into | night

rùn wù xì wú shēng
**润物细无声。**
moisten | thing | fine | no | sound

### Spring Night Happy Rain

*Du Fu*

Good rain falls in spring,
when everything grows and birds sing.
Wind brings rain unnoticed at night,
moistening everything silently in the moonlight.

*(Translated by Dr. X. Zhou and T. Gourdon)*

In this poem the poet brings to our attention the importance of wind and rain to the life on earth, often unnoticed by people. It gives us a sense of appreciation for the nature of earth around us.

*By Dr. X. Zhou*

## 悯 农
### Saluting the Farmer

李 绅 （772—846）

**锄禾日当午，**
hoe | grain | sun | when | midday

**汗滴禾下土。**
sweat | drop | grain | down | soil

**谁知盘中餐，**
who | know | plate | in | food

**粒粒皆辛苦。**
every grain | all | hard work

## Saluting the Farmer

*Li Shen*

Hoeing away the weeds in the midday heat,

sweat dripping onto the soil.

Where does this food come from that we eat?

Every morsel of grain is wrested with hard toil.

(*Translated by Dr. X. Zhou & T. Gourdon*)

This poem delivers a profound message about the hardship faced by farmers to put food on everybody's table. The moral is that we should not only be respectful and grateful to farmers but also appreciate every morsel of food we eat.

*By Dr. X. Zhou*

## 16 望庐山瀑布
### Watching the Waterfall on Mount Lu

李白（701—762）

rì zhào xiāng lú shēng zǐ yān
**日照香炉生紫烟，**
sun | shine | incense | pot | give rise to | purple | mist

yáo kàn pù bù guà qián chuān
**遥看瀑布挂前川。**
far away | watch | waterfall | hang | front | river

fēi liú zhí xià sān qiān chǐ
**飞流直下三千尺，**
fly | flow | vertically | down | three | thousand | foot

yí shì yín hé luò jiǔ tiān
**疑是银河落九天。**
wonder | be | silver | river | fall | nine | sky

### Watching the Waterfall on Mount Lu

*Li Bai*

Sun shines through the incense purple smoke,
watching in the distance a waterfall sparkling in the sunlight.
Flow flying down three thousand feet to splash and soak,
can it be the Milky Way falling from its infinite height?

(*Translated by Dr. X. Zhou & T. Gourdon*)

This poem captures the poet's imagination as he sits calmly in the mist of incense and beautiful scenery, watching the water cascade down the mountain sparkling in the sunlight giving him the feeling of the heavens coming down to earth.

*By Dr. X. Zhou*

## jiāng xuě
# 江 雪
**Snow on the River**

liǔ zōng yuán
柳宗元（773—819）

qiān shān niǎo fēi jué
**千 山 鸟 飞 绝，**
thousand | mountain | bird | fly | no more

wàn jìng rén zōng miè
**万 径 人 踪 灭。**
ten thousand | path | people | trace | disappear

gū zhōu suō lì wēng
**孤 舟 蓑 笠 翁，**
lonely | boat | palm coat | straw hat | old man

dú diào hán jiāng xuě
**独 钓 寒 江 雪。**
alone | fishing | cold | river | snow

### Snow on the River
*Liu Zongyuan*

A thousand mountains no birds high or low,
ten thousand paths human footprints nowhere to behold.
One lonely fisherman in palm hat and coat,
alone fishing the cold river among the ice and snow.

(*Translated by Dr. X. Zhou & T. Gourdon*)

In this poem the poet captures the serenity of nature on a winter's day, and the resilience of an old man fishing on a snow-covered river, braving the elements of nature and enjoying a moment of peace and tranquillity, a beautifully written poem indeed.

*By Dr. X. Zhou*

## 枫桥夜泊
### fēng qiáo yè bó
**Maple Bridge Night Mooring**

张 继（约715—约779）
zhāng jì

月落乌啼霜满天，
yuè luò wū tí shuāng mǎn tiān
moon | drop | raven | cry | frost | full | sky

江枫渔火对愁眠。
jiāng fēng yú huǒ duì chóu mián
river | maple | fishing | fire | facing | worry | sleep

姑苏城外寒山寺，
gū sū chéng wài hán shān sì
Gusu | town | outside | cold | hill | temple

夜半钟声到客船。
yè bàn zhōng shēng dào kè chuán
night | middle | bell | sound | arrive | guest | boat

# Maple Bridge Night Mooring

*Zhang Ji*

The moon drops as the ravens' cry echoes across the frosty sky,
fisherman under maples, fire blazing on worried face rubs sleepy eye.
Gusu Town the Cold Hill Temple outside,
midnight bell sounds arrival of a guest ferry at the riverside.

*(Translated by Dr. X. Zhou & T. Gourdon)*

    This poem describes a mid-night view of a fishing town, with the moon fading and ravens crying under a frosty sky. Fishing men's lights shining on the river, fires blazing on the bank. There is a guest ferry slowly approaching the town. The poet creates a real life scene with his magical pen.

*By Dr. X. Zhou*

## 长安秋望
### Autumn View in Chang'an

杜 牧（803—852）

lóu yǐ shuāng shù wài
**楼倚霜树外，**
tower | lean | frost | tree | outside

jìng tiān wú yì háo
**镜天无一毫。**
mirror | sky | no | one | inch

nán shān yǔ qiū sè
**南山与秋色，**
south | mountain | and | autumn | colour

qì shì liǎng xiāng gāo
**气势两相高。**
spirit | vigour | both | each other | high

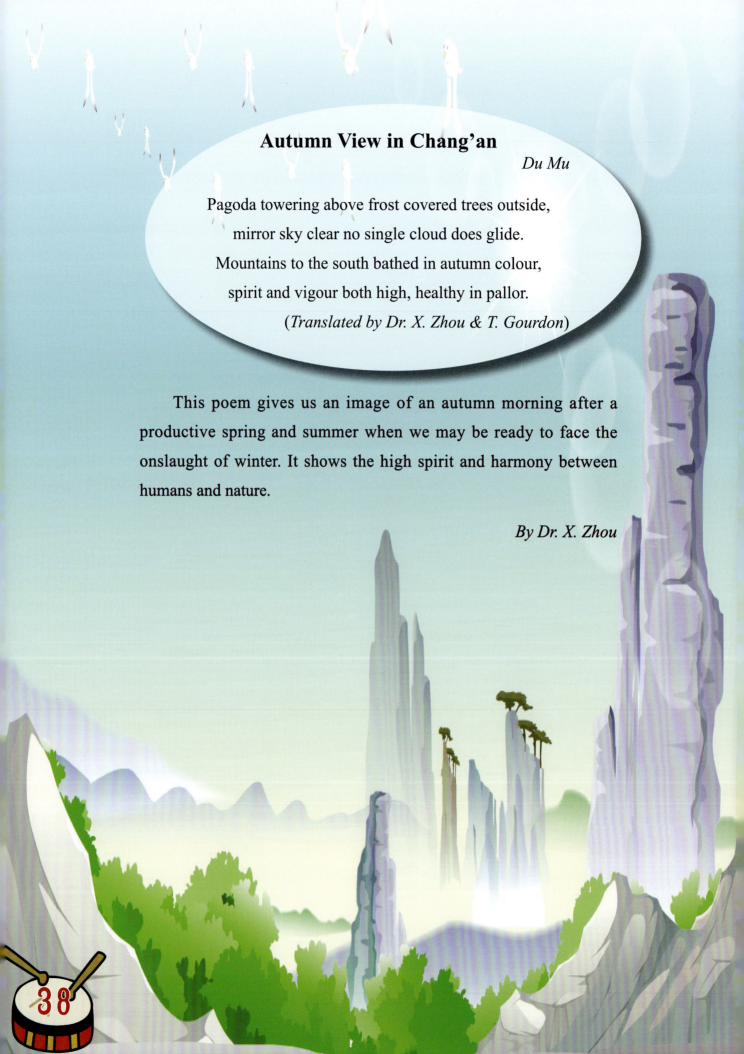

## Autumn View in Chang'an
*Du Mu*

Pagoda towering above frost covered trees outside,
mirror sky clear no single cloud does glide.
Mountains to the south bathed in autumn colour,
spirit and vigour both high, healthy in pallor.

*(Translated by Dr. X. Zhou & T. Gourdon)*

This poem gives us an image of an autumn morning after a productive spring and summer when we may be ready to face the onslaught of winter. It shows the high spirit and harmony between humans and nature.

*By Dr. X. Zhou*

# 20. 九月九日忆山东兄弟
### Remembering Shangdong Brothers on 9th of 9th

王维 (wáng wéi) (701—761)

独在异乡为异客，
alone | in | foreign | place | as | foreign | guest

每逢佳节倍思亲。
each | meet | good | festival | double | think of | relatives

遥知兄弟登高处，
distant | know | brothers | climb | high | place

遍插茱萸少一人。
all over | pick and arrange | wild flower | missing | one | person

**Remembering Shangdong Brothers on 9th of 9th**
*Wang Wei*

Alone as a stranger in a foreign town,
at festival time my thoughts turn around
to my family more than once.
Knowing that far away my brothers prance,
over high mountains picking wild flowers,
one person is missing during these happy hours.

*(Translated by Dr. X. Zhou and T. Gourdon)*

This poem captures the poet's strong feelings towards his family, especially his brothers when he was far away from them, during festival seasons. The first two lines of this poem are often quoted throughout Chinese-speaking communities by all who traveled away from home and families. So it is a well-known poem recited by people young and old.

*By Dr. X. Zhou*

## 望月怀远
### Moonlight Thoughts

张九龄 (678—740)

hǎi shàng shēng míng yuè
**海 上 生 明 月,**
sea | on | born | bright | moon

tiān yá gòng cǐ shí
**天 涯 共 此 时。**
sky | edge | together | this | moment

qíng rén yuàn yáo yè
**情 人 怨 遥 夜,**
loved | person | complain | remote | night

jìng xī qǐ xiāng sī
**竟 夕 起 相 思。**
throughout | night | start | each other | think of

## Moonlight Thoughts

*Zhang Jiuling*

Upon the sea the bright moon shines,
far away alone a loved one pines.
Emotions stirred by the night horizon's soothing lines
wonderful feelings of love and hope combine,
dusk brings warm thoughts of you my love in dreamtime.

*(Translated by Dr. X. Zhou & T. Gourdon)*

This poem is about the poet's feeling for his loved one far away on a full moon night as the moon rises and shines on the sea at dusk. In his mind he is yearning for the gentle caress of his loved one. Although we may be far apart from our loved ones, we can still see the same moon above wherever we are.

*By Dr. X. Zhou*

## 别董大
### Farewell to Dong Da

<sup>gāo</sup> <sup>shì</sup>
高 适（706—765）

qiān lǐ huáng yún bái rì xūn
**千里黄云白日曛，**
thousand | mile | yellow | cloud | white | sun | dusky

běi fēng chuī yàn xuě fēn fēn
**北风吹雁雪纷纷。**
north | wind | blow | wild goose | snow | in succession

mò chóu qián lù wú zhī jǐ
**莫愁前路无知己，**
not | worry about | front | path | no | know | oneself

tiān xià shuí rén bù shí jūn
**天下谁人不识君？**
sky | under | who | people | not | know | you

## Farewell to Dong Da

*Gao Shi*

Yellow clouds stretch for a thousand miles
basking under the white sun's smiles,
north wind blows wild geese like snowflakes.
No fear of the path ahead with no bosom friends,
under the sky all will know good genteels.

*(Translated by Dr. X. Zhou & T. Gourdon)*

This poem expresses the poet's friendship and encouragement to Dong Da, who is about to travel alone to places he has never been to before. The poet encourages him to face the road ahead without fearing the unknown but to think positively about his journey forward. The last two sentences are famous quotes that mean if you are a genuine person, a kind gentleman, you will be understood and respected by everyone wherever you go.

*By Dr. X. Zhou*

## 23 送灵澈
### sòng líng chè
### On Parting with Lingche

刘长卿（709—780）

cāng cāng zhú lín sì
**苍苍竹林寺，**
dark green | bamboo | forest | temple

yǎo yǎo zhōng shēng wǎn
**杳杳钟声晚。**
distant | bell | sound | late

hè lì dài xié yáng
**荷笠带斜阳，**
carry | bamboo hat | with | slanting | sun

qīng shān dú guī yuǎn
**青山独归远。**
green | mountain | alone | return | far away

# On Parting with Lingche
*Liu Changqing*

Vast temple, surreal amid the dark green bamboo,
the distant ring of the temple bell carries to.
Two friends parting in the evening dew,
bamboo hat on back setting sun casting shadows,
to green mountains far away alone one goes.

(*Translated by Dr. X. Zhou and T. Gourdon*)

This is a friendship poem between two poets, one is a monk living in a peaceful and remote temple in the mountains, away from the human corruptions and sufferings, and the other is a talented poet who travels around to capture nature's beauty. This poem is very simple but paints a beautiful picture of mountains and bamboo forests with a setting sun casting shadows on his friend as the bells in a distance call him back. The poet was deeply touched at that moment by the serenity and beauty of nature.

*By Dr. X. Zhou*

## 赠汪伦
### To Wang Lun

李 白（701—762）

lǐ bái chéng zhōu jiāng yù xíng
李白乘舟将欲行，
Li Bai | take | boat | about to | go

hū wén àn shàng tà gē shēng
忽闻岸上踏歌声。
suddenly | hear | bank | on | step | song | sound

táo huā tán shuǐ shēn qiān chǐ
桃花潭水深千尺，
peach | blossom | pond | water | deep | thousand | foot

bù jí wāng lún sòng wǒ qíng
不及汪伦送我情。
not | as | Wang Lun | see off | me | feeling

## To Wang Lun

*Li Bai*

Li Bai on a river boat about to set sail,
suddenly hears on the river bank
singing and dancing lively and hale.
Peach Blossom Pond a thousand feet deep,
not as deep as Wang Lun's friendship
that strengthens each time when we meet.

(*Translated by Dr. X. Zhou & T. Gourdon*)

This is a friendship poem written by Li Bai, one of the most famous poets during the Tang Dynasty. He was about to sail away on a boat alone, but suddenly he heard his friend singing on the river bank as a farewell, thus he was deeply touched and wrote this poem to express his feelings for his friend, deeper than the one-thousand-foot depth of the water in Peach Blossom Pond.

*By Dr. X. Zhou*

## 咏柳
### An Ode to the Willow

贺知章（659—744）

碧玉妆成一树高，
green | jade | decorate | become | one | tree | tall

万条垂下绿丝绦。
ten thousand | measure word | hang | down | green | silk | ribbon

不知细叶谁裁出，
not | know | tiny | leaf | who | cut | out

二月春风似剪刀。
second | month | spring | wind | like | scissors

### An Ode to the Willow

*He Zhizhang*

Jade green leaves decorate one tall tree,
ten thousand hanging branches
green and silky flowing free.
How did such fine shaped leaves get cut out?
February wind like scissors over the brae.

(*Translated by Dr. X. Zhou and T. Gourdon*)

In this poem we see a beautiful picture of a willow tree with vivid green leaves hanging down and swaying quietly in the wind. The poet captures the mood of the moment cleverly by personalising the tree and the spring wind to give the reader a real image of the scene.

*By Dr. X. Zhou*

## 26 梅花 (méi huā)
### Plum Blossoms

王安石 (wáng ān shí) (1021—1086)

**墙 角 数 枝 梅,**
qiáng jiǎo shù zhī méi
wall | corner | several | branch | plum blossom

**凌 寒 独 自 开。**
líng hán dú zì kāi
facing | cold | alone | oneself | flowering

**遥 知 不 是 雪,**
yáo zhī bú shì xuě
far away | know | not | be | snow

**为 有 暗 香 来。**
wèi yǒu àn xiāng lái
for | there is | hidden | fragrance | come

## **Plum Blossoms**

*Wang Anshi*

Several plum blossoms blooming
in the corner near the wall,
facing cold winter alone in flower.
I know from far away they are not snow at all,
there are hidden fragrances such aromatic power.
(*Translated by Dr. X. Zhou & T. Gourdon*)

This poem describes the famous plum blossoms flowering in winter, announcing the on-coming spring. Their unique beauty and fragrance permeating throughout the country create a peaceful and harmonious atmosphere. The plum blossoms symbolize the deep, unadulterated and noble personality of the poet.

*By Dr. X. Zhou*

## 27 春望 (chūn wàng)
**Spring Watch**

杜甫(dù fǔ)（712—770）

guó pò shān hé zài
**国破山河在，**
country | broken | mountain | river | exist

chéng chūn cǎo mù shēn
**城春草木深。**
city | spring | grass | tree | deep

gǎn shí huā jiàn lèi
**感时花溅泪，**
touched | time | flower | splash | tear

hèn bié niǎo jīng xīn
**恨别鸟惊心。**
hate | part | bird | shock | heart

## Spring Watch

*Du Fu*

The Kingdom is broken yet the mountains still stand magnificently,
rivers still flow unconcerned towards the sea,
my city amongst spring grass and forest trees stands proudly.
Sad emotions flood my eyes and the flowers too seem to splash tears,
people gone like flocking birds taking flight
my parting from this land burns my heart.

(*Translated by Dr. X. Zhou and T. Gourdon*)

In this poem the poet expresses his deep feelings for his war-torn country and his hope for the future peace. He sees the resilience of nature against all odds and his own sense of loss in terms of his ruined and desolate hometown. He finds consolation in the unchanged natural surroundings which shows how life continues on regardless of human greed and stupidity.

*By Dr. X. Zhou*

## 黄鹤楼
### 送孟浩然之广陵
**A Farewell at Yellow Crane Pagoda**

李白（701—762）

gù rén xī cí huáng hè lóu
**故人西辞黄鹤楼，**
old | person | west | farewell | yellow | crane | pagoda

yān huā sān yuè xià yáng zhōu
**烟花三月下扬州。**
mist | flower | third | month | go down | Yangzhou

gū fān yuǎn yǐng bì kōng jìn
**孤帆远影碧空尽，**
lonely | sail | far away | shadow | blue | sky | end

wéi jiàn cháng jiāng tiān jì liú
**唯见长江天际流。**
only | see | long | river | sky | edge | flow

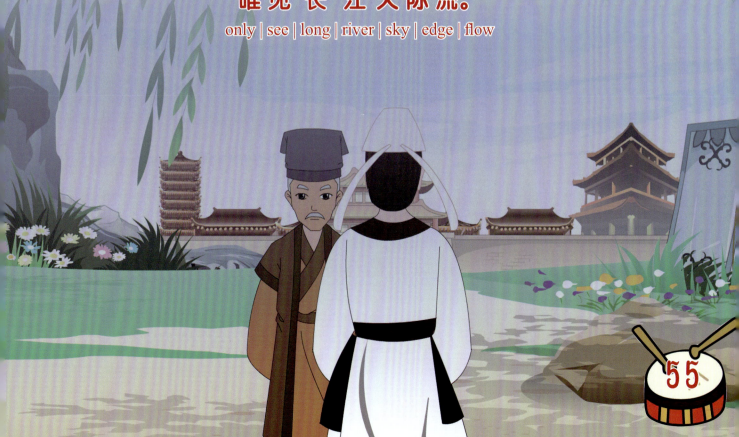

### A Farewell at Yellow Crane Pagoda

*Li Bai*

To the west of Yellow Crane Pagoda an old friend bids farewell,
travelling to Yangzhou as the March mists swirl.
The shadow of the lonely sail fades into the distance
under the empty blue sky,
now one can only see the Yangtze River
below the empty horizon flowing by.
(*Translated by Dr. X. Zhou & T. Gourdon*)

This poem expresses the tranquillity and emotional feelings of a moment when an old friend says farewell, and sails off on a new journey. The poet feels the emotions of a parting of a friend and also accounts the peacefulness of the scene.

*By Dr. X. Zhou*

## 黄鹤楼
### huáng hè lóu
**Yellow Crane Pagoda**

崔 颢（704—754）
cuī hào

昔 人 已 乘 黄 鹤 去，
xī rén yǐ chéng huáng hè qù
past | people | already | ride | yellow | crane | go

此 地 空 余 黄 鹤 楼。
cǐ dì kōng yú huáng hè lóu
this | place | empty | remaining | yellow | crane | pagoda

黄 鹤 一 去 不 复 返，
huáng hè yí qù bú fù fǎn
yellow | crane | once | go | not | again | return

白 云 千 载 空 悠 悠。
bái yún qiān zǎi kōng yōu yōu
white | cloud | thousand | year | empty | remote in time

晴 川 历 历 汉 阳 树，
qíng chuān lì lì hàn yáng shù
fine | river | clear | Hanyang | tree

芳 草 萋 萋 鹦 鹉 洲。
fāng cǎo qī qī yīng wǔ zhōu
fragrant | grass | luxuriant | parrot | island

日 暮 乡 关 何 处 是？
rì mù xiāng guān hé chù shì
sun | dusk | hometown | pass | which | place | be

烟 波 江 上 使 人 愁。
yān bō jiāng shàng shǐ rén chóu
mist | wave | river | on | make | people | worry

### Yellow Crane Pagoda

*Cui Hao*

Past ancestors already by the yellow crane borne
the Yellow Crane Pagoda empty
as ancestors from the earth were torn.
The sky with only white clouds vacant a thousand years
fine clear view over the vast plain to the Hanyang trees,
fragrant grass on Parrot Island swaying silently in the breeze.
Sunset over the countryside where is the safe haven?
Hidden perhaps amongst the forest trees.
A wavy mist forms over the river foreboding unsettled times,
people yearn for home with troubled minds.

(Translated by Dr. X. Zhou & T. Gourdon)

This poem reminds us of our own mortality as we think of the people who have long passed away yet still live within us. The clear view, fragrant grass and sunset are there for all today but tomorrow who knows. Thus the spirits wane and we long for the normality of home. The poet expresses his nostalgia through a vivid description of a natural scenery.

*By Dr. X. Zhou*

## dēng yōu zhōu tái gē
## 登 幽 州 台 歌
### Climbing Youzhou Pagoda

chén zǐ áng
陈子昂（661—702）

qián bú jiàn gǔ rén
前 不 见 古 人，
front | not | see | ancient | person

hòu bú jiàn lái zhě
后 不 见 来 者。
back | not | see | forthcoming | person

niàn tiān dì zhī yōu yōu
念 天 地 之 悠 悠，
think of | heaven | earth | of | remote in space

dú chuàng rán ér tì xià
独 怆 然 而 涕 下。
alone | feel sad | like that | so | tears | drop down

# Climbing Youzhou Pagoda
*Chen Zi'ang*

Ancient ancestors and the renowned lost in the past,
cannot foresee future heroes, no deed will last.
Thinking of the earth, the sky boundless and infinite,
alone, feeling sad, tears drop no foresight.
(*Translated by Dr. X. Zhou and T. Gourdon*)

This poem expresses the poet's reminiscence over the past renowned heros and looking forward he is unable to foresee the future heroes. He is disappointed to be born in an age where he found his talents and loyalty to the country not appreciated. He wrote this poem during his struggle to find his own way to excel in his contribution to the people and country at that time.

*By Dr. X. Zhou*

## 31

### 马诗 (mǎ shī)
### An Ode to the Horse

李贺 (lǐ hè)（790—816）

dà mò shā rú xuě
**大漠沙如雪，**
big | desert | sand | look like | snow

yān shān yuè sì gōu
**燕山月似钩。**
Yan | mountain | moon | look like | hook

hé dāng jīn luò nǎo
**何当金络脑，**
which | when | gold | net | brain

kuài zǒu tà qīng qiū
**快走踏清秋。**
quickly | go | ride | clear | autumn

## An Ode to the Horse

*Li He*

Desert sand glistering like snow,
hook like moon over Yan Mountain below.
When will the horse be fitted with the gold bridle
that glitters in the moonlight,
ready to gallop on a crystal clear autumn night.
Ride! Gallop to battle with all your might.

*(Translated by Dr. X. Zhou & T. Gourdon)*

In this poem, the poet captures a peaceful moment in the moonlight with his horse standing quietly nearby about to be saddled up and ridden over the desert into battle. The first two lines of this poem have been frequently quoted throughout the years for the vision they cast of that autumn night in the desert.

*By Dr. X. Zhou*

## 忆江南 yì jiāng nán
**Recalling River South**

白居易 bái jū yì (772—846)

jiāng nán hǎo
江南好,
river | south | good

fēng jǐng jiù céng ān
风景旧曾谙。
scenery | old days | still | familiar

rì chū jiāng huā hóng shèng huǒ
日出江花红胜火,
sun | out | river | flower | red | than | fire

chūn lái jiāng shuǐ lǜ rú lán
春来江水绿如蓝,
spring | come | river | water | green | like | blue

néng bú yì jiāng nán
能不忆江南?
can | not | recall | river | south

### Recalling River South

*Bai Juyi*

South of River good memories stirred
old familiar scenery unblurred.
Sunrise on riverside flowers
redder than fire in the dawning hours.
Green blue algae on river
heralds spring coming hither,
who could forget the River's South?

(*Translated by Dr. X. Zhou & T. Gourdon*)

    In this poem the poet paints a vivid picture of the beauty of Jiangnan—South of the famous Yangtze River, the green water in the river and beautiful flowers on the river bank during spring. The third and fourth lines of this poem are often quoted in Chinese literature to describe the natural beauty of the countryside.

*By Dr. X. Zhou*

## 33 海内存知己
### Bosom Friends across the Seas

wáng bó
王 勃（649—676）

hǎi nèi cún zhī jǐ
海内存知己，
sea | within | exist | know | oneself

tiān yá ruò bǐ lín
天涯若比邻。
sky | edge | as if | next door | neighbour

wú wéi zài qí lù
无为在歧路，
no need | at | branch | road

ér nǚ gòng zhān jīn
儿女共沾巾。
son | daughter | together | wet | towel

**Bosom Friends across the Seas**
*Wang Bo*

Bosom friends oceans will not part,
distant skies still like close neighbours.
Lost at parting roads with heavy heart,
pointles crying like children into wet towels.
*(Translated by Dr. X. Zhou & T. Gourdon)*

    This is a very famous poem, as it reflects the strength of friendship—a true friend is a friend who is always there for you even when far apart. It shows that there is no need to be sad when parting a friend, as real friendship will never die.

*By Dr. X. Zhou*

# 词语表
# Vocabulary

## A

| | | | |
|---|---|---|---|
| 安 | ān | peaceful; peace | 19 |
| 谙 | ān | familiar | 32 |
| 岸 | àn | bank | 7, 24 |
| 暗 | àn | hidden | 26 |

## B

| | | | |
|---|---|---|---|
| 八 | bā | eight | 1 |
| 白 | bái | white | 2, 7, 9, 10, 22, 29 |
| 白鹭 | báilù | egret | 10 |
| 百 | bǎi | hundred | 12 |
| 半 | bàn | half; middle | 18 |
| 报 | bào | to return | 6 |
| 北 | běi | north | 22 |
| 倍 | bèi | double; more than | 20 |
| 比 | bǐ | to compare | 33 |
| 碧 | bì | green; blue | 25, 28 |
| 遍 | biàn | all over; everywhere | 20 |
| 别 | bié | to part with; to say goodbye | 12, 22, 27 |
| 鬓 | bìn | temples | 3 |
| 拨 | bō | to paddle | 2 |
| 波 | bō | wave | 2, 29 |
| 泊 | bó | to moor | 10, 18 |

| | | | |
|---|---|---|---|
| 不 | bù | not | 1, 3, 5, 7, 8, 22, 24, 25, 26, 29, 30, 32 |
| 布 | bù | cloth | 16 |

## C

| | | | |
|---|---|---|---|
| 裁 | cái | to cut | 25 |
| 采撷 | cǎixié | to pick up | 11 |
| 彩 | cǎi | colourful | 7 |
| 餐 | cān | food; meal | 15 |
| 残 | cán | to wither; to die | 12 |
| 蚕 | cán | silkworm | 12 |
| 苍 | cāng | dark green; blue | 23 |
| 草 | cǎo | grass | 6, 8, 27, 29 |
| 层 | céng | storey; floor | 9 |
| 曾 | céng | not long after | 32 |
| 插 | chā | to insert; to pick and arrange | 20 |
| 长 | cháng | long | 19, 28 |
| 长安 | Cháng'ān | name of city, ancient capital of China | 19 |
| 长江 | Cháng Jiāng | Yangtze River | 28 |
| 成 | chéng | to become | 12, 25 |
| 城 | chéng | city; town | 7, 18, 27 |
| 乘 | chéng | to take; to ride | 24, 29 |
| 迟 | chí | late | 6 |
| 尺 | chǐ | a foot | 16, 24 |
| 重 | chóng | layer | 7 |
| 愁 | chóu | to worry | 18, 22, 29 |
| 出 | chū | out | 25, 32 |
| 锄 | chú | to hoe | 15 |

| 处 | chù | place | 3, 5, 13, 20, 29 |
| 川 | chuān | river | 16, 29 |
| 船 | chuán | boat | 10, 18 |
| 窗 | chuāng | window | 10 |
| 床 | chuáng | bed | 4 |
| 怆 | chuàng | to feel sad | 30 |
| 吹 | chuī | to blow | 8, 22 |
| 垂 | chuí | to hang down | 25 |
| 春 | chūn | spring | 5, 6, 8, 11, 12, 14, 25, 27 |
| 慈 | cí | kind | 6 |
| 辞 | cí | to say goodbye; to farewell | 7, 28 |
| 此 | cǐ | this | 11, 21, 29 |
| 从 | cóng | from | 3 |
| 衰 | cuī | to turn grey | 3 |
| 翠 | cuì | green | 10 |
| 村 | cūn | village | 13 |
| 存 | cún | to exist | 33 |
| 寸 | cùn | an inch | 6 |

# D

| 大 | dà | big; huge | 3, 31 |
| 带 | dài | to carry; with | 23 |
| 当 | dāng | when; right at the time | 14, 15, 31 |
| 刀 | dāo | knife | 25 |
| 到 | dào | to; until; to arrive | 12, 18 |
| 得 | dé | <particle> (used after a verb or an adjective to express possibility or capability) | 6 |

| | | | |
|---|---|---|---|
| 登 | dēng | to climb | 9, 20, 30 |
| 低 | dī | to lower | 4 |
| 滴 | dī | to drop | 15 |
| 地 | dì | earth; place; ground | 4, 29, 30 |
| 弟 | dì | younger brother | 20 |
| 帝 | dì | an emperor; a king | 7 |
| 钓 | diào | to go fishing | 17 |
| 东 | dōng | east | 10, 12, 20 |
| 董大 | Dǒng Dà | name of a person | 22 |
| 豆 | dòu | bean | 11 |
| 独 | dú | alone; lonely | 17, 20, 23, 26, 30 |
| 断 | duàn | to break | 13 |
| 对 | duì | face to face | 18 |
| 多 | duō | many | 5, 11 |
| 多少 | duōshǎo | how many | 5 |

## E

| | | | |
|---|---|---|---|
| 鹅 | é | goose | 2 |
| 儿 | ér | son | 3, 33 |
| 儿女 | érnǚ | children | 33 |
| 而 | ér | therefore | 30 |
| 二 | èr | two; second | 25 |
| 二月 | èr yuè | February | 25 |

## F

| | | | |
|---|---|---|---|
| 发 | fā | to set out; to shoot out; to open up | 7, 11, 14 |
| 发生 | fāshēng | to happen | 14 |
| 帆 | fān | sail | 28 |
| 返 | fǎn | to return | 29 |

| 方 | fāng | just; only | 12 |
| 芳 | fāng | fragrant | 29 |
| 飞 | fēi | to fly | 1, 16, 17 |
| 纷 | fēn | numerous; in succession | 13, 22 |
| 风 | fēng | wind | 5, 8, 12, 14, 22, 25, 32 |
| 风景 | fēngjǐng | scenery; landscape | 32 |
| 枫 | fēng | maple | 18 |
| 逢 | féng | to meet; to come upon | 20 |
| 缝 | féng | to knit; to sew | 6 |
| 浮 | fú | to float | 2 |
| 复 | fù | again | 29 |

# G

| 改 | gǎi | to change | 3 |
| 干 | gān | dry | 12 |
| 感 | gǎn | to feel; feeling | 27 |
| 高 | gāo | tall; high | 19, 20, 25 |
| 歌 | gē | to sing | 2, 24, 30 |
| 个 | gè | measure word | 10 |
| 更 | gèng | more; again | 9 |
| 共 | gòng | together | 21, 33 |
| 钩 | gōu | hook | 31 |
| 姑苏 | Gūsū | name of a town | 18 |
| 孤 | gū | lonely; alone | 17, 28 |
| 古 | gǔ | ancient | 30 |
| 故 | gù | former; old | 4, 28 |
| 挂 | guà | to hang | 16 |
| 关 | guān | pass | 29 |

| | | | |
|---|---|---|---|
| 鹳雀 | guànquè | stork | 9 |
| 光 | guāng | light | 4 |
| 广陵 | Guǎnglíng | name of a place | 28 |
| 归 | guī | to return | 6, 23 |
| 国 | guó | country | 11, 27 |
| 过 | guò | to pass | 7 |

## H

| | | | |
|---|---|---|---|
| 海 | hǎi | sea | 9, 21, 33 |
| 含 | hán | to contain | 10 |
| 寒 | hán | cold | 17, 18, 26 |
| 寒山 | Hánshān | name of a temple | 18 |
| 汉阳 | Hànyáng | name of a place | 29 |
| 汗 | hàn | sweat | 15 |
| 行 | háng | line | 10 |
| 毫 | háo | inch | 19 |
| 好 | hǎo | good; nice; fine | 14, 32 |
| 禾 | hé | standing grain | 15 |
| 何 | hé | a question word | 3, 13, 29 |
| 河 | hé | river | 9, 16, 27 |
| 荷 | hè | to carry; to load | 23 |
| 鹤 | hè | crane | 28, 29 |
| 恨 | hèn | to hate | 27 |
| 红 | hóng | red | 2, 11, 32 |
| 后 | hòu | behind; back | 30 |
| 忽 | hū | suddenly | 24 |
| 花 | huā | flower; blossom | 1, 5, 12, 13, 24, 26, 27, 28, 32 |
| 怀 | huái | to keep in mind; to yearn for | 21 |

| | | | |
|---|---|---|---|
| 还 | huán | to return | 7 |
| 黄 | huáng | yellow | 9, 10, 22, 28, 29 |
| 黄河 | Huáng Hé | Yellow River | 9 |
| 黄鹂 | huánglí | oriole | 10 |
| 灰 | huī | ash | 12 |
| 晖 | huī | sunshine | 6 |
| 回 | huí | to return; to go back | 3 |
| 魂 | hún | soul; spirit | 13 |
| 火 | huǒ | fire | 8, 18, 32 |

## J

| | | | |
|---|---|---|---|
| 及 | jí | to reach; as | 24 |
| 几 | jǐ | several | 11 |
| 己 | jǐ | oneself | 22, 33 |
| 际 | jì | edge | 28 |
| 佳 | jiā | good; nice | 20 |
| 家 | jiā | family; home | 3, 13 |
| 间 | jiān | in between; among | 7 |
| 剪 | jiǎn | to cut (with scissors) | 25 |
| 剪刀 | jiǎndāo | scissors | 25 |
| 见 | jiàn | to see | 1, 3, 12, 28, 30 |
| 溅 | jiàn | to splash | 27 |
| 江 | jiāng | river | 7, 17, 18, 28, 29, 32 |
| 将 | jiāng | to be going to | 24 |
| 角 | jiǎo | corner | 26 |
| 皆 | jiē | all | 1, 15 |
| 节 | jié | season; festival | 13, 14, 20 |
| 借 | jiè | to borrow; to lend | 13 |

| | | | |
|---|---|---|---|
| 巾 | jīn | towel; handkerchief | 33 |
| 金 | jīn | gold | 31 |
| 尽 | jìn | end; empty | 8, 9, 12, 28 |
| 惊 | jīng | to frighten; to surprise; to shock | 27 |
| 景 | jǐng | view | 32 |
| 径 | jìng | path | 17 |
| 竟 | jìng | throughout | 21 |
| 静 | jìng | quiet | 4 |
| 镜 | jìng | mirror | 19 |
| 九 | jiǔ | nine | 1, 16, 20 |
| 酒 | jiǔ | alcoholic; wine | 13 |
| 酒家 | jiǔjiā | bar; inn | 13 |
| 旧 | jiù | old | 32 |
| 举 | jǔ | to raise | 4 |
| 句 | jù | sentence | 10 |
| 炬 | jù | torch | 12 |
| 绝 | jué | empty; no more | 17 |
| 绝句 | juéjù | a poem of four lines | 10 |
| 觉 | jué | to be aware of | 5 |
| 君 | jūn | gentleman | 11, 22 |

## K

| | | | |
|---|---|---|---|
| 开 | kāi | to open; to bloom | 26 |
| 看 | kàn | to look at | 16 |
| 客 | kè | visitor; guest | 3, 18, 20 |
| 空 | kōng | sky; empty | 28, 29 |
| 恐 | kǒng | afraid | 6 |
| 枯 | kū | to wither; to die | 8 |

| | | | |
|---|---|---|---|
| 快 | kuài | quick; quickly | 31 |

## L

| | | | |
|---|---|---|---|
| 蜡 | là | wax | 12 |
| 来 | lái | to come | 3, 5, 11, 26, 30 |
| 老 | lǎo | old | 3 |
| 泪 | lèi | tear | 12, 27 |
| 离 | lí | to leave; to go away from | 3 |
| 离离 | lí lí | clear; clearly | 8 |
| 里 | lǐ | mile | 7, 9, 10, 22 |
| 力 | lì | force; strength | 12 |
| 历 | lì | clear; clearly | 29 |
| 笠 | lì | a straw hat | 17, 23 |
| 粒 | lì | measure word for grain | 15 |
| 两 | liǎng | two; both | 1, 7, 10, 19 |
| 邻 | lín | neighbour | 33 |
| 林 | lín | forest | 23 |
| 临 | lín | before; to be about to | 6 |
| 灵澈 | Língchè | name of a person | 23 |
| 岭 | lǐng | mountain | 10 |
| 凌 | líng | facing | 26 |
| 陵 | líng | hill | 7 |
| 流 | liú | to flow | 9, 16, 28 |
| 柳 | liǔ | willow | 10, 25 |
| 六 | liù | six | 1 |
| 楼 | lóu | building; pagoda; tower | 9, 19, 28, 29 |
| 庐山 | Lú Shān | Mount Lu | 16 |
| 芦 | lú | reed | 1 |

| | | | |
|---|---|---|---|
| 炉 | lú | pot | 16 |
| 路 | lù | road | 13, 22, 33 |
| 绿 | lǜ | green | 2, 25 |
| 络 | luò | net | 31 |
| 落 | luò | to fall; to drop | 5, 16, 18 |

# M

| | | | |
|---|---|---|---|
| 马 | mǎ | horse | 31 |
| 满 | mǎn | full | 18 |
| 毛 | máo | feather; hair | 2, 3 |
| 梅 | méi | plum | 26 |
| 每 | měi | each | 20 |
| 门 | mén | door; gate | 10 |
| 孟浩然 | Mèng Hàorán | name of a person | 28 |
| 密 | mì | tight | 6 |
| 眠 | mián | to sleep | 5, 18 |
| 灭 | miè | to disappear | 17 |
| 悯 | mǐn | pity; to show sympathy | 15 |
| 明 | míng | bright | 4, 13, 21 |
| 鸣 | míng | bird singing | 10 |
| 莫 | mò | not; don't | 22 |
| 漠 | mò | desert | 31 |
| 母 | mǔ | &lt;formal&gt; mother | 6 |
| 木 | mù | tree | 27 |
| 目 | mù | eye; vision | 9 |
| 牧 | mù | shepherd | 13 |
| 暮 | mù | dusk | 29 |

## N

| | | | |
|---|---|---|---|
| 乃 | nǎi | then | 14 |
| 南 | nán | south | 11, 19, 32 |
| 难 | nán | difficult; hard | 12 |
| 脑 | nǎo | brain | 31 |
| 内 | nèi | within; in | 33 |
| 能 | néng | can | 32 |
| 念 | niàn | to think of | 30 |
| 鸟 | niǎo | bird | 5, 17, 27 |
| 农 | nóng | farmer | 15 |
| 女 | nǚ | female; daughter | 33 |

## O

| | | | |
|---|---|---|---|
| 偶 | ǒu | accidentally; once in a while | 3 |

## P

| | | | |
|---|---|---|---|
| 盘 | pán | plate | 15 |
| 片 | piàn | piece (measure word for snowflakes) | 1 |
| 破 | pò | broken; to destroy | 27 |
| 瀑 | pù | waterfall | 16 |
| 瀑布 | pùbù | waterfall | 16 |

## Q

| | | | |
|---|---|---|---|
| 七 | qī | seven | 1 |
| 萋 | qī | luxuriant | 29 |
| 歧 | qí | (of roads) fork; branch | 33 |
| 歧路 | qílù | crossroad | 33 |
| 起 | qǐ | to start; to begin | 21 |

| | | | |
|---|---|---|---|
| 气 | qì | air; spirit | 19 |
| 千 | qiān | thousand | 1, 7, 9, 10, 16, 17, 22, 24, 29 |
| 前 | qián | front | 4, 16, 22, 30 |
| 潜 | qián | to dive | 14 |
| 墙 | qiáng | wall | 26 |
| 桥 | qiáo | bridge | 18 |
| 亲 | qīn | relative | 20 |
| 青 | qīng | blue; green | 10, 23 |
| 轻 | qīng | light | 7 |
| 清 | qīng | clear | 2, 13, 31 |
| 清明 | Qīngmíng | Qingming Festival | 13 |
| 情 | qíng | feeling; emotion | 21, 24 |
| 情人 | qíngrén | loved one; lover | 21 |
| 晴 | qíng | fine; clear | 29 |
| 穷 | qióng | to end; poor | 9 |
| 秋 | qiū | autumn | 10, 19, 31 |
| 曲 | qū | bent; bending | 2 |
| 去 | qù | to go | 29 |

## R

| | | | |
|---|---|---|---|
| 然 | rán | so; like that | 30 |
| 人 | rén | person; people | 13, 17, 20, 22, 28, 29, 30 |
| 日 | rì | sun; day | 7, 9, 15, 16, 20, 22, 29, 32 |
| 荣 | róng | to flourish | 8 |
| 如 | rú | like; as if | 31 |
| 入 | rù | to enter; into | 1, 9, 14 |

| 润 | rùn | to moisten | 14 |
|---|---|---|---|
| 若 | ruò | as if | 33 |

## S

| 三 | sān | three; third | 1, 6, 16, 28 |
|---|---|---|---|
| 三月 | sān yuè | March | 28 |
| 色 | sè | colour | 19 |
| 沙 | shā | sand | 31 |
| 山 | shān | mountain | 7, 9, 17, 18, 19, 20, 23, 27 |
| 山东 | Shāndōng | name of a province | 20 |
| 上 | shàng | on; to fly up; up | 4, 6, 8, 9, 10, 13, 21, 24, 29 |
| 烧 | shāo | to burn | 8 |
| 少 | shǎo | few; little; to be missing | 5, 20 |
|  | shào | young | 3 |
| 身 | shēn | body | 6 |
| 深 | shēn | deep | 24, 27 |
| 生 | shēng | to grow; to be born; to give rise to | 8, 11, 14, 16, 21 |
| 声 | shēng | sound | 5, 7, 14, 18, 23, 24 |
| 胜 | shèng | better than; more than | 32 |
| 诗 | shī | poem | 31 |
| 十 | shí | ten | 1 |
| 时 | shí | time; when | 12, 13, 14, 21, 27 |
| 识 | shí | to know | 3, 22 |
| 使 | shǐ | to make; to cause | 29 |
| 始 | shǐ | to begin | 12 |
| 势 | shì | force; vigour | 19 |
| 是 | shì | to be | 4, 16, 26, 29 |

| 手 | shǒu | hand | 6 |
| 书 | shū | to write; book | 3 |
| 树 | shù | tree | 19, 25, 29 |
| 数 | shù | number; several | 26 |
| 霜 | shuāng | frost | 4, 18, 19 |
| 谁 | shuí/shéi | who | 6, 15, 22, 25 |
| 水 | shuǐ | water | 2, 24 |
| 丝 | sī | silk | 12, 25 |
| 思 | sī | to think of; thought | 4, 11, 20, 21 |
| 死 | sǐ | to die; death | 12 |
| 四 | sì | four | 1 |
| 寺 | sì | temple | 18, 23 |
| 似 | sì | like; as if | 25, 31 |
| 送 | sòng | to see sb. off | 23, 24, 28 |
| 随 | suí | to follow; to go with | 14 |
| 岁 | suì | year (of age) | 8 |
| 蓑 | suō | palm leaf coat | 17 |

## T

| 踏 | tà | to step on; to ride | 24, 31 |
| 台 | tái | pagoda | 30 |
| 潭 | tán | pond | 24 |
| 绦 | tāo | silk ribbon | 25 |
| 桃 | táo | peach | 24 |
| 啼 | tí | to sing; to cry | 5, 7, 18 |
| 题 | tí | topic; title | 12 |
| 涕 | tì | tear | 30 |
| 天 | tiān | sky; heaven | 2, 10, 16, 18, 19, 21, 22, 28, 30, 33 |

| | | | |
|---|---|---|---|
| 天下 | tiānxià | the world | 22 |
| 条 | tiáo | measure word for tree branches | 25 |
| 童 | tóng | child | 3, 13 |
| 头 | tóu | head | 4 |
| 土 | tǔ | soil; earth | 15 |

## W

| | | | |
|---|---|---|---|
| 外 | wài | outer; outward; outside | 18, 19 |
| 晚 | wǎn | late | 23 |
| 万 | wàn | ten thousand | 1, 7, 10, 17, 25 |
| 汪伦 | Wāng Lún | name of a person | 24 |
| 望 | wàng | to look; to watch from a distance | 4, 16, 19, 21, 27 |
| 为 | wéi | as | 20, 33 |
| | wèi | because | 26 |
| 唯 | wéi | only | 28 |
| 闻 | wén | to hear | 5, 24 |
| 问 | wèn | to ask | 3, 13 |
| 翁 | wēng | old man | 17 |
| 我 | wǒ | I; me | 24 |
| 乌 | wū | raven | 18 |
| 无 | wú | no; not; without | 3, 12, 14, 19, 22, 33 |
| 无为 | wúwéi | no need | 33 |
| 吴 | wú | the Kingdom of Wu | 10 |
| 五 | wǔ | five | 1 |
| 午 | wǔ | noon; midday | 15 |
| 物 | wù | thing; substance; object | 11, 14 |

## X

| | | | |
|---|---|---|---|
| 夕 | xī | sunset; night | 21 |

| | | | |
|---|---|---|---|
| 西 | xī | west | 10, 28 |
| 昔 | xī | past | 29 |
| 喜 | xǐ | happy; to like | 14 |
| 细 | xì | fine; tiny | 14, 25 |
| 下 | xià | below; down; under | 15, 16, 22, 25, 28, 30 |
| 线 | xiàn | thread | 6 |
| 乡 | xiāng | hometown; countryside; village | 3, 4, 20, 29 |
| 相 | xiāng | each other | 3, 11, 12, 19, 21 |
| 香 | xiāng | incense; fragrance | 16, 26 |
| 向 | xiàng | towards | 2 |
| 项 | xiàng | neck | 2 |
| 小 | xiǎo | small; little | 3 |
| 晓 | xiǎo | dawn | 5 |
| 笑 | xiào | to smile; to laugh | 3 |
| 斜 | xié | slant | 23 |
| 心 | xīn | heart | 6, 27 |
| 辛苦 | xīnkǔ | hard work; hardship | 15 |
| 行 | xíng | to travel; to walk; to go | 6, 13, 24 |
| 杏 | xìng | apricot | 13 |
| 兄 | xiōng | elder brother | 20 |
| 兄弟 | xiōngdì | brother | 20 |
| 雪 | xuě | snow | 1, 10, 17, 22, 26, 31 |
| 曛 | xūn | dusky | 22 |

**Y**

| | | | |
|---|---|---|---|
| 涯 | yá | margin; limit; edge | 21, 33 |
| 烟 | yān | smoke; mist | 16, 28, 29 |

| | | | |
|---|---|---|---|
| 燕山 | Yān Shān | Mount Yan | 31 |
| 言 | yán | to say; to speak | 6 |
| 雁 | yàn | wild goose | 22 |
| 扬州 | Yángzhōu | name of a city | 28 |
| 阳 | yáng | sun | 23 |
| 遥 | yáo | distant; remote; far away | 13, 16, 20, 21, 26 |
| 杳 | yǎo | distant; out of sight | 23 |
| 野 | yě | wild | 8 |
| 叶 | yè | leaf | 25 |
| 夜 | yè | night | 4, 5, 14, 18, 21 |
| 一 | yī | one; once; single | 1, 8, 9, 10, 19, 20, 25, 29 |
| 衣 | yī | clothes | 6 |
| 依 | yī | to go along with | 9 |
| 疑 | yí | to doubt; to wonder | 4, 16 |
| 已 | yǐ | already | 7, 29 |
| 倚 | yǐ | to lean against | 19 |
| 忆 | yì | to recall; to remember | 20, 32 |
| 亦 | yì | also | 12 |
| 异 | yì | strange; foreign | 20 |
| 意 | yì | mind | 6 |
| 音 | yīn | sound; accent | 3 |
| 吟 | yín | to chant; to recite | 1, 6 |
| 银 | yín | silver | 16 |
| 银河 | Yínhé | Milky Way | 16 |
| 鹦鹉 | yīngwǔ | parrot | 29 |
| 影 | yǐng | shadow | 28 |
| 咏 | yǒng | to recite a poem; to chant | 2, 25 |

| | | | |
|---|---|---|---|
| 幽州 | Yōuzhōu | name of a place | 30 |
| 幽州台 | Yōuzhōu Tái | name of a pagoda | 30 |
| 悠 | yōu | remote in time or space | 29, 30 |
| 游 | yóu | to travel | 6 |
| 有 | yǒu | to have | 13, 26 |
| 又 | yòu | again | 8 |
| 余 | yú | remaining | 29 |
| 渔 | yú | fishing | 18 |
| 与 | yǔ | and | 19 |
| 雨 | yǔ | rain | 5, 13, 14 |
| 玉 | yù | jade | 25 |
| 欲 | yù | to want; to be about to | 9, 13, 24 |
| 原 | yuán | prairie | 8 |
| 猿 | yuán | ape | 7 |
| 远 | yuǎn | far away | 21, 23, 28 |
| 怨 | yuàn | to complain | 21 |
| 愿 | yuàn | to wish | 11 |
| 月 | yuè | moon; month | 4, 18, 20, 21, 25, 28, 31 |
| 云 | yún | cloud | 7, 22, 29 |

## Z

| | | | |
|---|---|---|---|
| 载 | zǎi | year | 29 |
| 在 | zài | to be at a place; to exist | 20, 27, 33 |
| 早 | zǎo | early morning; early | 7 |
| 赠 | zèng | to give sth. as a gift | 24 |
| 沾 | zhān | wet | 33 |
| 掌 | zhǎng | palm | 2 |

| 朝 | zhāo | early morning; dawn | 7 |
| 照 | zhào | to shine | 16 |
| 者 | zhě | person (used after an adjective or verb as a substitute for a person or a thing) | 30 |
| 之 | zhī | to; of | 28, 30 |
| 枝 | zhī | branch; measure word for plant | 11, 26 |
| 知 | zhī | to know | 5, 14, 15, 20, 22, 25, 26, 33 |
| 知己 | zhījǐ | bosom friend; best friend | 22, 33 |
| 直 | zhí | straight; vertically | 16 |
| 指 | zhǐ | to point at | 13 |
| 中 | zhōng | middle; in | 6, 15 |
| 钟 | zhōng | bell | 18, 23 |
| 舟 | zhōu | boat | 7, 17, 24 |
| 洲 | zhōu | islet; island | 29 |
| 茱萸 | zhūyú | name of a wild flower; cornel | 20 |
| 竹 | zhú | bamboo | 23 |
| 住 | zhù | to stop | 7 |
| 妆 | zhuāng | to decorate; to make up | 25 |
| 子 | zǐ | child | 6 |
| 紫 | zǐ | purple | 16 |
| 自 | zì | oneself | 26 |
| 踪 | zōng | trace | 17 |
| 走 | zǒu | to go; to walk | 31 |
| 最 | zuì | most | 11 |

# 作者简介

周晓康：1978年考入中国杭州大学（今浙江大学）外语系，获英国语言文学学士、硕士学位。1985年留校任教，在杭州大学中文系教对外汉语、公共英语、语言学概论等，同时进修中文系现代汉语研究生课程。1987年考入北京大学英语系，攻读英国语言文学博士学位，同时在北京大学中文系进修现代汉语和历史语言学。1989年赴澳，随后就读澳大利亚墨尔本大学语言学系，专业为西方语言学和系统功能语法，并于1998年获墨尔本大学语言学博士学位。1999年就读拉筹伯大学（La Trobe University）教育系，获教育学研究生文凭。2000年至今任教于墨尔本半岛文法学校（Peninsula Grammar），现任该校中文系主任。除此之外，1993年通过澳大利亚翻译局翻译资格考试，获得澳大利亚翻译局注册三级翻译资格。

在澳大利亚的对外汉语教学中最突出的成就为编写350余首语言教学歌谣，2008年12月获第9届国际汉语教学研讨会优秀示范课创新奖。2009年2月获新金山教育基金2008年全澳优秀中文教师奖。2009年9月由北京大学出版社出版的《晓康歌谣学汉语》第一集获美国国际最佳少年图书"月光奖"铜奖。2009年11月荣获澳大利亚维多利亚多元文化杰出贡献奖。2009年12月获中华儿童文化艺术促进会举办的"祖国，您好"美术书法摄影作文大展的美术作品"园丁奖"和作文指导"园丁奖"。2010年8月获第10届国际汉语教学研讨会优秀示范课创新奖。2011年3月，中国国家汉办隆重推出其精心挑选制作的《晓康歌谣》专辑，作为推荐教材正式上线。2011年

10月，周晓康、李晶博士合著的《晓康歌谣趣味故事》获美国国际最佳少年图书"月光奖"铜奖。同年12月，周晓康博士获中国侨办授予的海外华文教师优秀奖。2012年10月，周晓康博士与T. Gourdon合著的《丁丁迪米历险记》英汉读物获美国国际最佳少年图书"月光奖"金奖。2015年，教学视频《半岛中国情》获首届澳大利亚生活秀视频大奖赛三等奖。2016至2017年，《晓康歌谣学汉语》第三、第四集相继出版，从而完成这套独具一格的国际汉语教材全集。2017年11月，荣获全球北京大学优秀校友奖，以表彰其对海外汉语教学所作出的杰出贡献。2018年12月获澳大利亚维多利亚中文教师歌唱比赛创新奖和演唱第三名。2019年6月浙江科技学院人文与国际教育学院聘其为客座教授。2020年7月被聘为浙江大学汉语国际教育专业硕士业界导师。

在过去的二十年里，周晓康博士以其别具一格、引人入胜的歌谣汉语教学法在海内外备受瞩目。多年来，她在澳大利亚孜孜不倦传授中华语言与文化，笔耕不辍，著书立说，在众多国际会议上作学术报告、教学示范，深受欢迎。

# About the Author

Dr. Xiaokang Zhou: Commenced her higher education in 1978 and graduated in 1985 from Department of Foreign Languages, Hangzhou University（now Zhejiang University）, China, with a Bachelor degree and a Master of Arts degree in the English Language and Literature. She was employed by the same university to teach Chinese as a Foreign Language, English, General Linguistics and studied the postgraduate course of Modern Chinese in the Chinese Department. Having passed the entry examinations she was accepted by Peking University as a Ph.D. candidate in the English Department in 1987. During her Ph. D. candidature in Peking University, she studied Modern Chinese and Historical Linguistics in the Department of Chinese. In 1989, she came to Australia as a visiting scholar and continued her Ph. D. study in the Department of Linguistics, the University of Melbourne, focusing on Western Linguistics and Systemic Functional Grammar, and received her Ph. D. degree in Linguistics from the University of Melbourne in 1998. In 1999 she studied in Department of Education of La Trobe University and received her Graduate Diploma in Education. She was employed to teach English as a Second Language as well as Chinese at Peninsula Grammar in 2000 and has been teaching there since then, as Head of Chinese now. Apart from Linguistics and Education, she also held a qualification as a NAATI (National Authority of Accredited Translators and Interpreters) Level 3 Mandarin-English translator after passing its qualifying examination in 1993.

The most significant contribution she made to the Chinese language education in Australia is the series of Dr. Zhou's Rhymes for learning Chinese (over 350 rhymes). In December 2008 she received the International Award for Excellence in Innovative Teaching of Chinese and was awarded the Most Excellent Chinese Teacher of 2008 by the Golden Land Education Foundations in February 2009.

Her book entitled *Dr Zhou's Rhymes for Learning Chinese* published by Peking University Press has won the Bronze Medal in the 2009 Moonbeam International Children's Book Awards in the USA.

Dr. Xiaokang Zhou received Victoria's Multicultural Award for Excellence 2009 in Australia. She also received a Teacher's Award in "Hello China" Grand Exhibition of Fine Arts, Calligraphy, Photography and Written Composition held in Beijing, China. In August 2010, Dr. Xiaokang Zhou was presented the International Award for Excellence in Innovative Teaching of Chinese at the 10th International Chinese Language Teaching Conference for the second time.

In March 2011, the State Council of Chinese Language (International) formally launched the Special Edition of *Dr. Zhou's Rhymes* selected by the committee as a recommended Chinese textbook online.

Dr Xiaokang Zhou 's another book *Dr Zhou's Fun Stories*, co-authored with Dr. J. Li, published by Peking University Press in 2011, won the Bronze Medal in the Moonbeam International Children's Book Awards in the USA in 2011. In December 2011, Dr. Zhou received the Excellent Overseas Chinese Teacher Award from the Overseas Chinese Council of the People's Republic of China. Her most recent book, *Adventures of Dingding and Damien*, co-authored with T. Gourdon, published by Peking University Press in 2012, won the Gold Medal in the Moonbeam International Children's Book Awards in the USA in 2012. Dr. Zhou's video entitled Peninsula Chinese Fun has won the 3rd Place in the 1st Australian Life Video Show Awards Competition in 2015. During 2016 to 2017, *Dr. Zhou's Rhymes for Learning Chinese* Book 3 and Book 4 were published, which means the completion of the whole set of this unique and innovative textbook for Chinese as a Second Language. Dr. Zhou was awarded the Excellent Alumnus of Peking University in November 2017 for her significant contributions to the Chinese Language Teaching overseas. In December 2018, Dr. Xiaokang Zhou won the Innovative Award as well as receiving the 3rd Place Award in the Victoria Chinese Teachers Singing Competition organized by the Chinese Language Teachers Association of Victoria, Australia. In June 2019 Dr. Xiaokang Zhou was appointed as Honorary Professor of the Humanity and International Education School of Zhejiang Science and Technology University,

China. She was appointed as the Honorary Supervisor of International Chinese Education Master of Arts Program by Zhejiang University in July 2020.

Dr Xiaokang Zhou has gained prominence over the past two decades for her commitment to the teaching of the Chinese language using innovative and engaging methods. She is a prolific author and a popular speaker at many international conferences.